ROUTE 66 LOST & FOUND

Mother Road Ruins and Relics — The Ultimate Collection

RUSSELL A. OLSEN

Voyageur Press

This book is dedicated to the memory of Dean Finmark—you are deeply
missed my friend—and to the memories of Lucie T. McMurtie
and Mary Lou Knudsen.

First published in 2011 by Voyageur Press, an imprint of MBI
Publishing Company, 400 First Avenue North, Suite 300, Minneapolis,
MN 55401 USA

The information in this book is true and complete to the best of our
knowledge. All recommendations are made without any guarantee
on the part of the author or Publisher, who also disclaims any liability
incurred in connection with the use of this data or specific details.

We recognize, further, that some words, model names, and
designations mentioned herein are the property of the trademark
holder. We use them for identification purposes only. This is not an
official publication.

Voyageur Press titles are also available at discounts in bulk quantity
for industrial or sales-promotional use. For details write to Special
Sales Manager at MBI Publishing Company, 400 First Avenue North,
Suite 300, Minneapolis, MN 55401 USA.

To find out more about our books, visit us online at
www.voyageurpress.com.

Library of Congress Cataloging-in-Publication Data

Olsen, Russell A., 1954–
 Route 66 lost & found : mother road ruins & relics, the ultimate
collection / Russell A. Olsen.
  p. cm.
 Reorganized, updated and expanded ed. of earlier work with same
title proper.
 Includes index.
 ISBN 978-0-7603-3998-5 (flexibound)
 1. West (U.S.)–Pictorial works. 2. United States Highway 66—Pictorial
works. 3. Roadside architecture–West (U.S.)–Pictorial works. 4.
Historic sites–West (U.S.)–Pictorial works. 5. Postcards–West (U.S.) 6.
West (U.S.)–Description and travel. 7. Olsen, Russell, A., 1954–Travel–
West (U.S.) I. Title. II. Title: Route 66 lost and found.
 F590.7.O533 2011
 978–dc22
                          2010053499

10   9   8   7   6   5   4   3   2   1

Printed in China

CONTENTS

ACKNOWLEDGMENTS

There are many people to thank for helping me with this book: I owe a great deal of gratitude to the people that allowed me access to their private postcard collections: Earl Cory, Laurel Kane, Jerry McClanahan, Jeff Meyer, Steven Rider, Jim Ross, Joe Sonderman, and Mike Ward.

I would like to thank the following for helping with research and or supplying vintage photos of many of the locations appearing in this book: Nick Adam, Kathy Anderson, Tim Burchett, Marion Clark, the late C. H. "Skip" Curtis, Linda Drake, Mike Dragovich, Janice Lauritzen, John Hockaday, Richard Mangum, Scott Piotrowski, the late Tom Teague, Bill Thomas, John Weiss, and Betty Wheatley. A big thumbs-up to Chris More and Zach Allred for allowing me access to the PG&E facility for the Red Rock Bridge photo. Thank you Brett Bather for technical assistance.

Special thanks to Russell Adams at Schulman Photo Lab in Hollywood, and a very special thank you to Mardjie and Vince Paradero for their outstanding black-and-white photo printing.

PREFACE

During many years of traveling Route 66 for pleasure or work, I have run across thousands of people who hold the road dear to their hearts and minds. Each one of these individuals offers their own unique look at Route 66 and a unique reason why it is so special to them.

Many look at the road as a form of nostalgia, hearkening back to a time that seems less complicated to them than today. Many couples looking to turn back time set out for that small café or diner where they fell in love; others seek out the quaint mom-and-pop motel where they spent their honeymoon. Maybe your connection to Route 66 is a trading post where Mom talked Dad into buying you that rubber tomahawk. All the time, I hear from people asking me about the location of "their" special place on Route 66.

Others see traveling down the Route 66 as form of relaxation, just taking in the sights along the way. When traveling our favorite highway, just the occasional glance out the window from time to time will reveal stark, visual contrasts in geography. As the pavement winds its way through a variety of striking landscapes, you will truly be amazed. From the deserts of California to the mountains of Arizona, the rolling hills of Missouri, and the flatlands of Illinois, somewhere along your journey, Route 66 provides whatever type of scenery you might favor. The Mother Road truly has it covered. Personally, that is what I love about traveling the road. Just driving, relaxing, and taking in the scenery—and maybe taking a few photos along the way.

Many other fans of the road take it upon themselves to act as custodians. Preservation of our beloved motels, gas stations, and cafés is certainly admirable. Most, if not all, of this hard work is performed on a volunteer basis, with the satisfaction of a job well done its single compensation. Volunteer groups along the entire route continue to fight to save and preserve our icons from destruction. There are literally hundreds of sights from Chicago to Los Angeles that we are in jeopardy of losing. Sometimes these volunteers win and sometimes they lose, but they are always fighting. My hat's off to you!

Other fans of Route 66 enjoy the social aspects of the road. The Route 66 community is widespread and includes folks from around the world. Numerous Route 66 festivals take place throughout the summer months in most of the eight states. These mostly informal get-togethers provide a great place to meet new friends and fans from around the globe. These festivals are also the perfect venue to relax and exchange information on upcoming Route 66 events or to reveal the location of that lost alignment or section of Portland cement that you finally discovered.

In addition, these events are a fantastic place to learn about the history of Route 66. Many are attended by historians who graciously take the time to set up informative displays. Others bring along amazing antique postcard collections that most of us just dream of owning. Finally, these Route 66 events provide a chance for you to meet the authors of your favorite Route 66 books (this being one of course) and creators of favorite Route 66 art.

Whether you enjoy history, socializing, driving, photography, collecting antiques, preservation, or art, what it boils down to is this: Route 66 has a place for you and you have a place on Route 66. It does not matter why you are there, only that you are there. So please get out on the road and discover what it is about the most famous highway in the world that gets you excited. Experience the Mother Road and its people, and you will get hooked—I promise you.

The Route 66 community and I lost several supporters and friends over the last couple of years, including Lucie T. McMurtie, Mary Lou Knudsen, and Robert Waldmire. These were special people and true road warriors in every sense. They will be deeply missed by all.

This book is dedicated to their memory and to that of my old friend, Dean Finmark. A truer friend no one ever had.

At the turn of the century roads and highways in the state of Illinois were primitive at best and impossible to navigate at worst. The history and development of Route 66 in Illinois can be traced back to these primitive roads and trails. In 1915 the main artery between Chicago and St. Louis was known as the Pontiac Trail, named for the eighteenth century chief of the Ottawa tribe. The trail was officially marked that same year with mile-by-mile guideposts from Chicago to St. Louis (courtesy of the B. F. Goodrich Company) ensuring even the novice traveler of at least having a chance of arriving at the proper destination. In 1918 a bond issue was passed for construction of hard roads in Illinois. The Pontiac Trail was designated SBI 4 (State Bond Issue) and began at 48th and Ogden in the western Chicago suburb of Cicero. After years of politicking and bureaucratic red tape, most of the road was finally paved by 1924, and by 1926 it was entirely a "hard road." The American Association of State Highway Officials approved the road for a U.S. Route designation and in 1927 U.S. Highway 66 signs were posted along its entire length.

Over the years many major changes took place to the routing of Route 66 in Illinois. In 1933 the easternmost terminus was moved from Cicero farther east to the entrance of Grant Park at Jackson Boulevard in Chicago. Another change took place in 1955 when Jackson became a one-way street and the official starting point was moved one block north to Adams Street, making the official endpoint the intersection of Jackson and Lake Shore Drive. In 1931 the original routing that followed Illinois Route 4 from Springfield to Staunton was rerouted to the east from Springfield to Litchfield, continuing to Mt. Olive. Another realignment occurred in the early 1930s when the route through Joliet and Wilmington was changed to alternate status and primary Highway 66 was redirected through Plainfield then on to Gardner, where the two versions of the route merged. As commercial truck traffic swelled and automobile traffic exploded throughout the late 1940s and into the 1950s, two-lane 66 was constantly improved and updated, and by 1957 the route was by and large a four-lane highway. The added improvements helped solve the congestion and safety problems but were no cure; it became painfully evident that Route 66 was outdated. It was the beginning of the end of the Mother Road in Illinois. By the mid-1970s most of Route 66 had been replaced with the new and modern Interstate 55. On January 17, 1977, the Illinois Department of Transportation removed the signs from the easternmost terminus, marking the official end of Route 66 in Illinois.

Today's traveler can still find much of the charm of old Route 66 in Illinois as they drive south from the towering concrete caverns of downtown Chicago, to the suburbs of Cicero and La Grange, and on through plains towns like Godley, Gardner, Dwight, Odell, Cayuga, Pontiac, Chenoa, Towanda, Funks Grove, Atlanta, Broadwell, Glenarm, Farmersville, Litchfield, Hamel, and Mitchell. To some, these small communities may be little more than dots on a map, but make no mistake: every town, motel, service station, mechanic, café, waitress, and short-order cook along the highway played an important role in shaping the history of Route 66 in Illinois.

WISHING WELL MOTEL, LA GRANGE
c. 1946

The Wishing Well Motel was built by John Blackburn in 1941 at the corner of Route 66 (now Joliet Road) and Brainard Avenue, just 15 miles from the heart of downtown Chicago. When built, the motel consisted of 10 cabins, an office, and a small house out back. Blackburn later sold the property to the Bronsons, who in turn sold it to Emil and Zora Vidas in 1958. In 1960 the individual cabins were connected to increase capacity, and in 1983 the property underwent more remodeling with the addition of four units. A small house in back was also converted to guest quarters, upping the room count to 19.

For more than 60 years the Wishing Well treated its guests to a quiet, country-like atmosphere just out of shouting range of the big city. In the early 1960s the nearby Willowbrook Ballroom booked swing and dance bands for months at a time and the Wishing Well became a home away from home for the musicians. Members of the rock band Chicago were guests in the early 1970s, although Zora was admittedly quite hesitant about renting to "those kids with that long hair."

Emil Vidas passed away in 1985, and Zora, who took over as manager and caretaker, passed away in 2004. The 66-year-old motel was demolished in 2007.

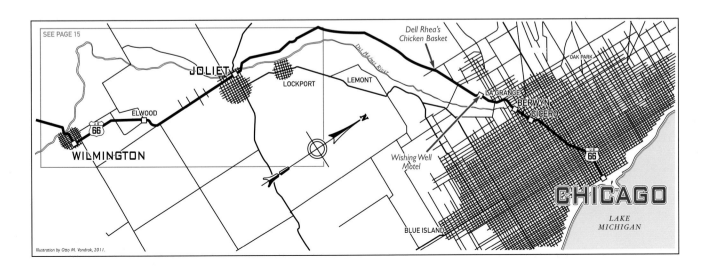

Illustration by Otto M. Vondrak, 2011.

DELL RHEA'S CHICKEN BASKET, WILLOWBROOK
c. 1946

Adjacent to the current location of Dell Rhea's Chicken Basket, a man named Irv Kolarik owned and operated a gas station where he also served up pie, coffee, and cold sandwiches at a small lunch counter. One day two local woman overheard Kolarik say owning a restaurant would be more to his liking and offered to teach him how to cook fried chicken if he would buy his chickens from them. A deal was struck and the rest, as they say, is history.

The chicken became so popular that he converted his two service bays into dining rooms. In June 1946 the business moved to its current location and became known as the Nationally Famous Chicken Basket. (Prior to 1946 the business was known both as Club Roundup and the Triangle Inn.) In one of the more elaborate schemes to attract customers to a roadside business, Kolarik had the restaurant's roof flooded during the winter months and hired skaters to perform there.

Spotlights aimed at the skaters created quite a scene at night.

The property changed ownership two times during the late 1950s and early 1960s. When four-lane Route 66 bypassed the Chicken Basket, the restaurant fell on hard times and was eventually repossessed. In 1963 Dell Rhea and his wife, Grace, bought the business from the bank and changed the name to Dell Rhea's Chicken Basket. Today the restaurant looks much as it did in 1946. The only alteration is an enclosed outdoor patio.

In June 1992 Dell Rhea's Chicken Basket was inducted into the Illinois Route 66 Hall of Fame. Rhea's son, Patrick, purchased the restaurant from his family in 1986 and is responsible for many of the tasty dishes served there today. Patrick notes that all dishes are prepared using the finest fresh ingredients, and that his chicken is marinated 24 hours before it's hand-breaded. Anyone hungry?

THE RIVIERA, GARDNER
c. 1946

Established in 1928 by James Girot, a businessman from nearby South Wilmington, the Riviera Restaurant and Tavern is located on Route 66 (now Route 53) 60 miles south of Chicago. Buildings from the towns of Gardner (a church) and South Wilmington (a coal mine office) were moved and combined on-site to form the Riviera, which during its heyday also featured a zoo, picnic grounds, and a swimming hole, with the picturesque Mazon River just a couple of yards away. At the height of its popularity, the Rivera's restaurant was located upstairs, serving homemade Italian food, chicken, steak, and seafood. The lower portion of the building was a tavern.

The Riviera is rich in Route 66 history and Chicago gangster lore.

Al Capone and his brother Ralph often wet their whistles in the downstairs speakeasy after checking on their stills in nearby Kankakee County. Gene Kelly was also a frequent customer. In 1933 a gasoline station was added but was eventually shut down. In 1972 Bob and Peggy Kraft purchased the Riviera from the Girots and have carried on the Riviera tradition of good food and drink. The restaurant and tavern are now both downstairs. The food is transferred from the upstairs kitchen via a dumbwaiter. Walking into the now-combined restaurant and tavern, visitors are instantly transported to another time when flappers and jazz music were the rage and the speakeasy was the place to get a drink and socialize with friends.

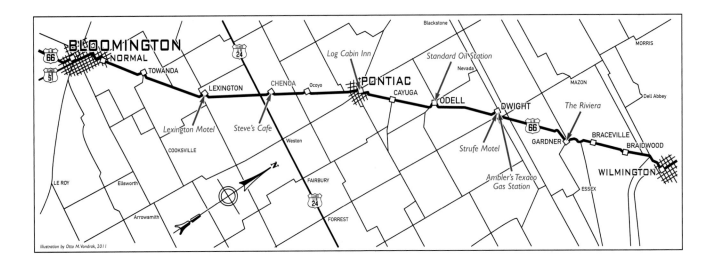

Illustration by Otto M. Vondrak, 2011

AMBLER'S TEXACO GAS STATION, DWIGHT
c. 1933

Jack Schore built the original structure at the corner of Route 66 and Illinois Route 17 with the help of his son Paul in 1933. The station holds the honor of being one of the longest-operating service stations on all of Route 66. It uses a design commonly called the "domestic style" gas station that was developed by the Standard Oil Company in 1916. This neighborhood-friendly design stemmed from growing community opposition to the often-unsightly gas stations growing more common in and around towns during that time. It was an obvious effort to create gas stations that would blend in with their surrounding neighborhoods. This design also created a secure, homelike atmosphere that oil executives hoped would attract out-of-town travelers.

In 1936 Vernon VonQualon leased the property from Schore and operated the station for two years before turning it over to Basil "Tubby" Ambler, who operated the station from 1938 until 1965.

During the early 1940s Ambler added a service bay, allowing the business to offer service and repairs year-round. In 1965, Ambler sold the station to Earl Kochler, who in turn sold it to Royce McBeath. It changed hands one more time when McBeath sold it to Phil Becker on March 4, 1970. Becker had begun working there in 1964, just one year before Ambler sold to Kochler. One year after Becker purchased the station, Texaco abruptly stopped supplying the station its gasoline. Becker signed on with Marathon, and the station was known as Becker's Marathon Gas Station for over 26 years.

The station was listed on the National Register of Historic Places on November 29, 2001. Although it changed hands many times, Ambler's significant 27-year ownership prompted the station to be listed as Ambler's Texaco Gas Station. It's currently being restored to its 1940 appearance and will be utilized as a Route 66 interpretive center.

STRUFE MOTEL, DWIGHT
c. 1952

The Strufe Motel was built on the southwest end of Dwight, just south of the Ambler station. It began life as a gas station, built and owned by Martin and Mehta Paulsen, who had emigrated from Denmark. Sometime after the station was completed, the Paulsens built six tourist cabins out back and joined them together with a single roof, creating a carport for each cabin. During the time that Martin and Mehta owned the business, it was called Paulsen's Court.

John and Dorothy Strufe purchased the business in 1952 and renamed the complex the Strufe Motel. For the first couple of years, the Strufes worked and lived in the station with their son, Frederick, who was four years old when they purchased it. In 1959 they decided to discontinue the sale of gasoline. The pumps were removed, and the station was converted into a living space and an office for the motel. Eventually the carports were enclosed, creating four additional rooms and a large utility room. Brick veneer was used to cover the front and sides, giving the individual units the appearance of a single ten-unit building. Following the remodeling the name was changed to the Arrow Motel.

After the tragic death of the Strufes in an automobile accident in 1968, Frederick continued to operate the motel until 1973, when it was sold to Norris and Betty Ruff. The motel changed hands again in 1977 and 1989 when the William DuPont and James Moyemont families entered into a partnership. Michael Moyemont eventually bought out all the partners and is now sole owner of the property. The ten-unit motel has been converted into two apartments and sits quietly concealed behind new vinyl siding, which covers the old brick veneer.

STANDARD OIL STATION, ODELL
c. 1932

Built in 1932 by Patrick O'Donnell, this gas station sits on the southwest side of Odell in Livingston County, just a few yards from the fabled Mother Road. Like many of the gas stations in this part of the country, it was built using original plans developed by Standard Oil of Ohio in 1916. The basic design of the "domestic style" gas station, as it was dubbed, consisted of a simple houselike structure with an attached canopy. The Odell station featured Standard Oil products for many of its early years, but by 1940 it was distributing Phillips 66 through its pumps. Prior to 1952 the station discontinued selling Phillips 66 and switched allegiance to Sinclair. The last drop of gas sold at the station was Sinclair brand in 1967.

During the glory days of Route 66, competition among gas station owners was fierce. There were more than ten stations on the short stretch of Route 66 in and around Odell. To attract more business, O'Donnell added service bays in 1937. When the bypass appeared and other stations fell by the wayside from lack of business, the service bay proved to be the station's saving grace.

In 1952 Robert Close leased the station from O'Donnell and bought the property after O'Donnell's passing in 1967. Close and his family lived in a converted café adjacent to the filling station until the café burned down sometime in the 1970s. Close eventually began doing bodywork at the station and continued until the Village of Odell bought the property in 1999.

Efforts to have the historic Standard Oil Station listed on the National Register of Historic Places began in 1995 and were rewarded with the station's listing in November 1997. Preservation efforts began in earnest in 1998, when volunteers from the Route 66 Association of Illinois began working diligently to preserve this Route 66 icon for future generations. The beautifully restored filling station is currently operated as a museum and information center.

STEVE'S CAFÉ, CHENOA
c. 1950

The building that eventually housed Steve's Café was built in 1918 and was originally called Wahls Brothers. Steve's Café came about in the 1930s when new owner Steve Wilcox took over. People in the area still speak in reverence when referring to the pie and coffee served at Steve's. A Texaco service station was later added to the business. A canopy was added and the station was fully enclosed in the early 1970s. The Texaco station closed shortly thereafter and around 1975 that section of the building was turned into a bar called the Red Bird Lounge, named for the local Chenoa Red Birds high school sports teams. In 1975 Ken and Peg Sipe took over the building and

continued to serve home-cooked meals and "World Famous Pie." During the summers, Steve's Café sponsored Friday-night fish fries at the local park. Peggy desperately tried to keep the café open after her husband was killed in an auto accident but eventually had to close the doors in 1997 after 22 years in business. Since the café's closure it has seen service as a used-car lot and an antique shop. Les Stevens, a Chenoa police officer, says what he remembers most about Steve's was the "huge steak-and-eggs breakfast with potatoes and the works for $3.99." The old cafe currently sits quietly on old 66, clinging to its past and hoping for a future.

"The Finest Steaks Between Chicago and St. Louis"

STEVE'S CAFE INTERSECTION CITY 66 & 24 CHENOA, ILLINOIS

LEXINGTON MOTEL, LEXINGTON
c. 1950

Lexington was one of the first towns to be settled in McLean County. In 1828, John Patton and his family built a crude log cabin where they spent their first Illinois winter and thus became Lexington's first permanent residents. Although many families began to migrate to the area, the town wasn't officially laid out until 1837 when James Brown and Asahel Gridley took up the challenge.

U.S. Highway 66 came through town in 1926, and many smaller towns along the route had at least one motel in operation soon after Highway 66 was born, but it wasn't until 1950 that Lexington saw its first and only motel catering to travelers on the Mother Road. That was the year Carl Christianson and his son Richard built the Lexington Motel.

The back of the advertising postcard seen here brags of "18 good clean units—all modern" with "two good restaurants nearby." A Mobil Oil station operated by Allen Gleeson sat adjacent to the motel, ready to take care of any automotive needs guests of the Lexington Motel might have.

With the coming of Interstate 55, business waned and the motel was eventually forced to close its doors. Like many owners of older motels along Route 66, the owners of the Lexington Motel remodeled their units and converted the motel into a residential apartment complex. The Mobil Station that sat next door was also forced to close and was eventually torn down.

The outside appearance of the motel has changed little since it was built in 1950. As a matter of fact, the only clue that this is no longer a working 1950s motel is the absence of the Lexington Motel sign that once adorned one of the buildings.

DIXIE TRUCKERS HOME, McLEAN
c. LATE 1940s

J. P. Walters and his son-in-law, John Geske, built the Dixie Truckers Home in 1928 at the intersection of U.S. Routes 66 and 138 in McLean, Illinois. Housed in a rented garage, the first incarnation of the café had only a counter and six stools. Throughout its history, the Dixie Truckers Home has been constantly improved and remodeled. In the late 1930s six tourist cabins were added and eventually the café was expanded to serve 60 people. In 1965 a grease fire in the kitchen, aided by wooden exhaust ducts, destroyed the café. Amazingly, the tourist cabins and gas pumps were unscathed. In fact, that very evening, the gas pumps were back in business and one of the cabins

was pressed into service as a temporary home for the café. The new Dixie Truckers Home reopened two years later with the capacity to serve 250 hungry travelers. The Dixie Truckers Home was not only consistently ranked among the nation's top 10 truck stops, serving customers with that southern hospitality its name implied, it was also home to the Route 66 Hall of Fame and Museum. At the time of this writing, the longtime family-owned truck stop was sold to a company based in Providence, Rhode Island, which planned to change the Dixie's name to Dixie Travel Plaza.

PALMS GRILL CAFÉ, ATLANTA
c. 1934

James Robert Adams opened the Palms Grill Café in August 1934, boasting "home cooking, quick service and courteous treatment." Adams was born just outside of Atlanta but moved to Los Angeles after serving in World War I. He shuttled back and forth between Los Angeles and Atlanta but spent a majority of his time in California. He named the café in reference to his time spent in that state. In fact, the interior was decorated as homage to a restaurant Adams frequented near his home in Los Angeles.

The café occupied the north half of a building known as the Downey Building, which was built after the Civil War in 1867. With five tables and two counters, the seating capacity for the café was about 30.

From the beginning the "The Grill," as it was locally known, was more than just a source of good food. Soon after its opening, the café developed into an integral part of Atlanta's social scene. Many Atlanta teenagers got their first taste of employment waiting tables or grilling short orders there. Behind the kitchen at the rear of the building was a dance hall, where locals would gather on Wednesday nights to cut loose and socialize. The dance hall was also used to host large private gatherings and parties.

In January 1940 the Palms Grill Café became a designated Greyhound Bus stop. A small light at the bottom of the neon sign out front signaled bus drivers when passengers were waiting to board. From the late 1940s through the 1950s, the café became *the* place for Atlanta High School students to meet and eat. In the late 1960s, however, after Highway 66 traffic was routed away from the center of town, the Palms Grill Café served up its final dinner. The last owner of the Downey Building, John Hawkins, remodeled the interior into a living and work space. Upon his passing in 2002, the Hawkins family donated the building to the Atlanta Public Library and Museum. The vintage interior of the Palms Grill Café is currently being restored. The original Downey Building was listed on the National Register of Historic Places in 2004.

REDWOOD MOTEL, LINCOLN
c. 1965

Construction of the Redwood Motel began in 1955 and its first guests were welcomed in 1956. Built by Wilfred and Dorothy Werth, the Redwood sat conveniently at the junction of Routes 66, 10, and 21, with 15 rooms and a small living quarters attached to the main building. The exterior of the motel was originally constructed of stone and redwood, but by 1960 so many stones were falling off the walls that Wilfred decided to brick the entire exterior. The cost to stay at the Redwood in 1956 was $5 for a single and $8 for a double. When television was installed the rates were raised to $6 and $10, respectively.

In 1934, 22 years prior to opening the motel, Wilfred had built a Standard Oil station on the same corner. Wilfred proudly states that he had the "first gasoline pumps in the state that showed the dollars and cents through the small windows on the pumps." Wilfred, who turned 87 in 2003, adds that he and Dorothy "had fun" owning the motel but sold it in 1963 when Ruth Buckles made an offer he couldn't refuse. The station was sold in 1991 and is today a Quick Lube. The original motel sign was torn down after high winds ripped off a few letters, says current lessee Sherman West, and was replaced with a new sign in November 2002. Sherman and wife Joan have plans to renovate the entire motel, hoping to make it a "must" stop for travelers on Old 66.

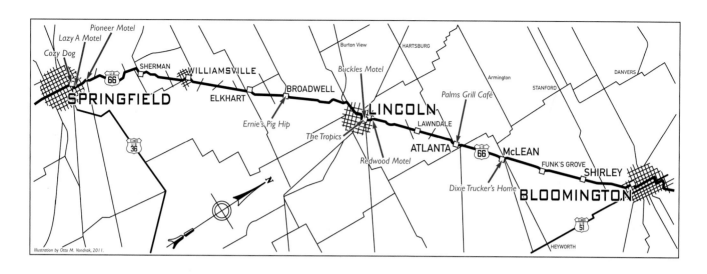

Illustration by Otto M. Vondrak, 2011.

BUCKLES MOTEL, LINCOLN
c. 1949

Route 66's original path through Lincoln wound its way through quiet residential neighborhoods and adjacent to the downtown business district. Around 1940, a beltline, or bypass, of 66 was constructed along the northern and western boundaries of the city. It was on this "Beltline 66" that the Buckles Motel was built.

Located on a small plot of land on the north side of Lincoln, the Buckles Motel was built by Paul and Ruth Buckles around 1949. The motel's original appearance was heavily influenced by the Spanish adobe style as seen in the photo. This architectural style was very common in the Southwest but somewhat unusual for this part of the country.

In the late 1950s, the motel was completely remodeled and upgraded to a more contemporary style. The unique Spanish-style office-and-home combination was also remodeled, eliminating any resemblance to the original architecture. A shingle and sloped roof replacing the flat roof was the most significant alteration.

The motel boasted of having "strictly modern units, central heating, [and] tub-shower combinations" with restaurants nearby.

The Buckles invested in many properties in and around Lincoln, including the Redwood Motel on Route 66 (see pages 36–37) in 1963.

When Interstate 55 was completed, the Route 66 bypass became Business 55 and is now known as Lincoln Parkway. The motel's office and home now serve as a private residence, while the motel units have been converted to monthly apartments. The buildings that once made up the Buckles Motel have so completely blended into the surrounding residential neighborhood that a first glance reveals nothing of their past. A truly hidden gem.

THE TROPICS, LINCOLN
c. 1956

The Tropics sits on the northeast corner of the intersection known locally as "the four corners" on a portion of Route 66 built just prior to World War II. This new section of roadway was designated "Beltline 66," and the intersection comprised U.S. 66, 10, and 121 and was situated just south of what was locally known as "Killer Corner."

The Tropics was built in 1950 by Vince Schwenoha, son of legendary John Schwenoha a.k.a. Coonhound Johnny. John got the nickname for his fondness of hunting raccoons with his four vicious coon dogs. John also ran a prohibition-era roadhouse just north of Lincoln on Route 66, aptly dubbed Coonhound Johnny's Roadhouse. In 1947, the structure was moved to downtown Lincoln where it became the local community recreation center and a popular hangout out for local kids.

After a tour of duty in the military, Vince returned to Lincoln and opened the Tropics. He named the restaurant in memory of the time he spent in the Hawaiian Islands while in the service.

One of the most popular items on the Tropics menu was a two-patty burger of the sort Vince first came across in California. The double burgers were selling like wildfire in the Golden State, so he brought the concept back to Lincoln and dubbed the borrowed burger the Tropicburger.

In the 1950s, Vince sold the Tropics to Lewis Johnson. Under Lewis' management, the Tropics became much more than a restaurant—it became the hangout for Lincoln residents and the host of choice for local clubs. Community and cultural events were often held at the Tropics, including a series of beauty pageants in the late 1950s. A local radio station would even broadcast from the Tropics on occasion.

Longtime owner Lewis Johnson leased the business in 1997 to James Letsos, who also owned a restaurant on Route 66 in Pontiac, Illinois. This arrangement only lasted until October 1999 when a lack of business forced Letsos to close.

The spring of 2001 saw the Tropics reopen for business under the ownership of Sam Dalipi. In 2005, however, the Tropics closed once again.

During its heyday, the Tropics was open from 7 a.m. to 1 a.m. daily and featured a coffee shop, dining room, and the Bamboo Cocktail Lounge. The jaw-dropping neon sign with glowing green palm tree still stands out front. Every time I see it at night, all I can think of is perching myself on a stool in the cocktail lounge and ordering a Mai Tai. Go figure.

ERNIE'S PIG HIP, BROADWELL
c. 1972

Ernie Edwards opened what would become the famous Pig Hip Restaurant in 1937 with three tables, a bar, $150 of borrowed money, and a desire to be his own boss. At first the restaurant was called the Harbor Inn because of a great deal Ernie found on wallpaper and restaurant glasses with a nautical theme. The name was shortlived. One day a hungry farmer came into the restaurant and spied a freshly baked ham on the stove. He pointed to the ham and said, "Give me a slice o' that pig hip." The rest, as they say, is history. Ernie applied for a patent on his sandwich (a generous helping of thinly sliced ham smothered with Pig Hip sauce) and copyrighted the name Pig Hip.

The sandwich was so popular that he opened two more restaurants in nearby towns but eventually closed them when he realized that managing two more Pig Hips was more than he had bargained for.

Ernie finally hung up his chef's hat and carving knife in 1991 after 54 years of serving up a local legend. With the help of the Illinois Route 66 Preservation Committee, Ernie's Pig Hip restaurant was transformed into a Route 66/Pig Hip Museum in late spring 2003, with 700 attending opening day. The Pig Hip's slogan, "The sandwich with the secret sauce: It made its way by the way it's made," was a fitting tribute to Ernie Edwards and his famous sandwich.

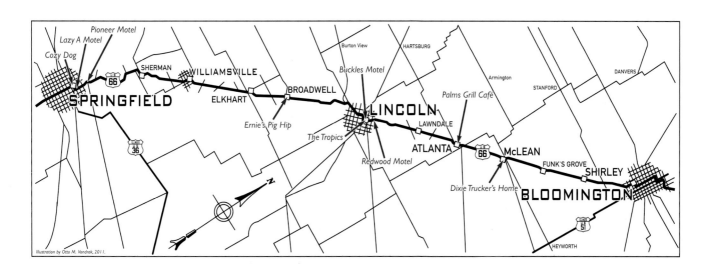

Illustration by Otto M. Vondrak, 2011.

PIONEER MOTEL, SPRINGFIELD
c. 1940s

The classic Pioneer Motel sits on the north end of Springfield, beckoning to cars passing by on historic 66. This small motel was built in the 1940s close to Route 66 and the Route 66 city bypass and was highly rated by AAA. The Pioneer initially consisted of 12 units arranged in the classic L-shape style, with parking in front of each room. Sometime after the original construction, an archway was built over the driveway at the front office for guest safety, and a living room was added to the office space. At one time a small motel existed adjacent to the Pioneer but was eventually purchased by the owners of the Pioneer. The added rooms increased the Pioneer's total guest rooms to 21. The motel currently rents many units out by the month but keeps a few open for overnight guests looking to spend the night at a vintage Route 66 motel. One of the current owners, Teresa Roberts, says plans are in the works to renovate the motel. This, she says, will "hopefully attract more interest to the Pioneer Motel from travelers and fans of Route 66." Although the motel has gone through several ownership changes over the years, the name was never changed and to this day the classic MOTEL sign tower above the office continues to greet guests.

LAZY A MOTEL, SPRINGFIELD
c. 1949

Situated on the north side of the city, this western ranch-style motel beckoned travelers who could not wait to catch a glimpse of America's West. For travelers heading back east after a fun-filled vacation, it was the perfect spot to experience one last taste of the West. The 16-unit motel would have looked right at home in Arizona or New Mexico. Even the name conjures images of a Southwest ranch. In Springfield, Illinois, it was surely unusual.

A member of the American Motor Hotel Association and recommended by AAA, the Lazy A boasted tile baths, locked garages, and most of all, being fireproof.

After the interstate came through, the Lazy A began to fade like a slow western summer sunset, and soon a lack of business forced its owners to close its doors. Eventually the motel was renovated and remodeled and served for years as an apartment complex. The structure then underwent another complete renovation and conversion to a small business park.

The old fencing, the wagon wheel decorations, and ranch-like atmosphere are all distant memories. The last time I drove past this old relic, I thought about its out-of-place architecture and the countless children in backseats clutching cowboy and Indian souvenirs from their recent vacations, begging to stop for the night—one last-ditch effort to relive the western adventures that remained fresh in their minds. On second thought, maybe the Lazy A was not so out of place after all.

COZY DOG DRIVE IN, SPRINGFIELD
c. 1950

Ed Waldmire Jr. and his friend Don Strand developed the Cozy Dog while stationed in Amarillo, Texas, during World War II. To earn extra money, Ed sold the new-fangled food—a delectable combination of a hot dog on a stick dipped in special batter and French-fried—at the USO club and at the base PX. The "Crusty Curs," as they were first known, quickly became a local favorite. After Ed's discharge from the military he introduced the "dogs" to the public at the 1946 Illinois State Fair; they were such a hit that Ed decided to sell his new fast food in his hometown of Springfield, Illinois.

The first Cozy Dog stand was opened at the Lake Springfield beach house on June 16 of that same year. At the insistence of his wife Virginia, who wondered who would eat something called a "Crusty Cur," Ed began kicking around ideas for a new name. After much painstaking thought, "Cozy Dog" was settled upon. A second Cozy Dog stand was opened on Ash and MacArthur in Springfield, and in 1950 Waldmire moved into a building that shared seating with the local Dairy Queen. In 1976, Ed's son Buz and daughter-in-law Sue leased the restaurant from Ed. After their divorce, Buz sold his half to Sue, who has run the restaurant ever since. The Cozy Dog moved to its current location at 2935 South 6th Street in 1996 and sits partially on the property of the former Route 66 landmark Lincoln Motel.

ART'S MOTEL AND RESTAURANT, FARMERSVILLE
c. 1955

In 1932 Art McAnarney and Marty Gorman became business partners, operating everything from speakeasies and gas stations to dance halls and casinos in and around Farmersville. In 1937 McAnarney decided to go it alone and sold his share of the business back to Gorman. McAnarney leased a building that once housed the two-story Hendricks Brothers' Café and Gas Station and went into business for himself. He continued operating a restaurant and gas station, as well as renting six cabins for overnight guests, until the building caught fire in 1952, destroying the second floor. The main-floor dining room was salvageable; McAnarney rebuilt the business, utilizing the old dining room and the foundation, but opted for a single-story structure.

McAnarney died in 1957, leaving the business to his sons, Elmer and Joe. By that time, two-lane Route 66 in Illinois was almost nonexistent, having given way to the new and updated four-lane version. In 1960 the sons added a 13-room L-shaped motel that still stands today. When Interstate 55 was completed in the mid-1970s, it ran right in front of the property. An exit for Farmersville was built, and, as luck would have it, Art's was conveniently located near the on/off ramp, averting what would otherwise have spelled the end of the business. Although Art's Motel and Restaurant continued to operate, as of this writing it's closed and looking for a new owner. In 1995 Art's was inducted in to the Illinois Route 66 Hall of Fame.

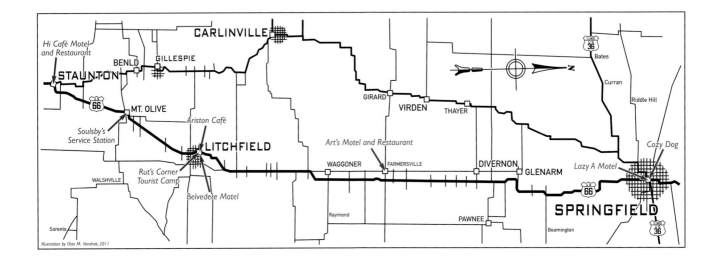

Illustration by Otto M. Vondrak, 2011

ARISTON CAFÉ, LITCHFIELD
c. 1935

Ariston Café, opened by Pete Adam in the town of Carlinville in 1924, consisted of a small café with a few gas pumps out front. In 1926, Route 66 was given official designation and routed through the small Illinois town, and Adam's business flourished. In 1931, however, Highway 66 was re-routed east through Litchfield and business suffered. Not one to give up, Pete moved the Ariston to Litchfield. Business boomed again and in 1935 he found it necessary to construct a larger building. This "new" café, which holds more than 100 hungry customers, stands today pretty much as it did when it was built almost 70 years ago. Over the years, 66 was rerouted several times through Litchfield. Each change made it necessary to move the front door of the restaurant to keep it facing the road. As fate would have it, with the last realignment the restaurant entrance wound up at the original front location.

The Ariston is a well-known stop along Route 66 and has been a family-run operation since opening its doors. Nick and Demi Adam are proud of the café's history and its connection with the Mother Road, and continue the fine tradition that began 80 years ago. "We continue to believe in offering the highest quality selection of food, while providing the first-rate service that you expect," they say, "and at a price that continues to bring our valued customers back time and time again."

Belvedere Motel and Café, Litchfield
ca. 1952

Vincenzo "James" and Albina Cerolla, seeing the potential for a roadside Highway 66 business, purchased several lots in Litchfield in the late 1920s and began their business in 1929 with a one-room, wood-frame gas station with a single pump. At the time, they partnered with the Johnson Oil Refining Company of Chicago (which later became the Horton Oil Company). As money permitted, the Cerollas expanded their business to include a motel and café, both built in 1936. The small four-unit motel was originally designed to include individual garages located between each unit. A new and larger gas station built of brick was also constructed, replacing the original around the same time.

The new four-lane 66 was completed through Litchfield in 1940. Located west of the original two-lane road and on the opposite side of the motel property, its position resulted in the need to reorient entrances to the business and construct new signage.

Vincenzo passed away in 1945, and Albina followed in 1949, at which time the property was willed to their daughter, Edith, and her husband, Lester "Curly" Kranich.

Around 1950, Lester and Edith remodeled the motel by enclosing the garages to make room for additional guest units. The interior of these units look much the same as they did after the remodel. The original plaster walls, ceilings, and wood floors, as well as original shower stalls, wall sinks, and toilets remain.

During the time of the remodeling, two additional buildings were added behind the gas station to the south of the original motel, each containing four units. Each new building housed both one- and two-bedroom units. (One of the new buildings can be seen in the lower left of the photo.) Lester and Edith also built a one-story residence on the property during the same time period. All this new construction proved one thing: demand for tourist facilities on Route 66 skyrocketed during the postwar years as people took to the road in droves. It was a golden era for the roadside businesses throughout the country.

With the completion of the interstate in the early 1970s, however, business tapered off. The gas station became the first victim and closed shortly after the opening of the interstate. Edith and Lester continued to successfully operate the motel and café until their retirement in 1975. The 1980s saw the property change hands several times until current owner, Yo Cho Hamric, bought it in 1989.

As of 2010, Hamric rented out the residence and occasionally rented out a room in the 1950s wing of the motel. The remaining motel units, café, and gas station are primarily used for storage.

RUT'S CORNER TOURIST CAMP, LITCHFIELD
c. 1929

Russell "Ruts" Brawley built Rut's Corner Tourist Camp just a few years after it was decided that Highway 66 would run through the town of Litchfield. A single row of gable-roofed cabins sat on one side of Brawley's property. A structure containing five guest units was positioned perpendicular to the cabins; for customers' convenience, each unit had a covered garage with a private entry. A community bathhouse was provided for guests of both the cabins and of the rooms.

A café was eventually added but burned to the ground in 1936. Olind McPherson, a one-time employee, remembers, "The fire was so hot that coins were melted together." The café was quickly rebuilt bigger and better, with room to serve upwards of 150 hungry guests. T-bone steak dinners were 40 cents.

"Rut's Corner was one of the busiest and most popular spots between Chicago and St. Louis," says McPherson. "The slot machines were the big thing." Brawley would say to him, "When a crowd gathers around the slot machines don't worry about cleaning up or anything. Just make sure the customers have change to feed the machines." McPherson also remembers galvanized wash basins of change so heavy that two men had to lift them. "That's how popular the slot machines were," he says.

A filling station was added later, making Rut's Corner a full-service tourist stop. Rut's closed sometime in the late 1950s. McPherson began cutting hair and has owned a barbershop for over 60 years. He remains in Litchfield and, at age 82, continues to cut hair. "I still work three days a week giving haircuts but now it's by appointment only," he says proudly.

RUT'S CORNER CAFE, ROUTE U. S. 66, LITCHFIELD, ILL.

SOULSBY'S SERVICE STATION, MOUNT OLIVE
c. 1926

Henry Soulsby was a southern Illinois coal miner by trade, following in his father's footsteps. Injury forced Soulsby to retire from mining sometime in the mid-1920s. In 1926, betting that the new U.S. Highway 66 would pass through Mount Olive, he used his life savings to purchase property on which he planned to build a gas station. With help from his young son, Russell, he proceeded to build a small, 30x12 structure of his own design. After high school, Russell joined his father in the business full time, while his sisters, Ola and Wilma, pitched in on a part-time basis. When Henry retired, Russell and Ola took over the daily operation of the station.

In 1937 the station was doubled in size but was never large enough for a repair bay. All repairs were performed outdoors on a ramp situated on the south side of the building. Following a stint in the military as a communications technician during World War II, Russell Soulsby returned to the station and quickly began utilizing his experience to repair radios and, later, televisions. After the interstate bypass was built in the late 1950s and automobile traffic dwindled, his television-repair business proved to be his mainstay. In 1991 Soulsby's discontinued the sale of gasoline but kept the station store open to sell soda, add the occasional quart of oil, and greet the growing number of tourists traveling the old road. In 1993 Soulsby closed his doors for good and sold the property in 1997 to Mike Dragovich in a public auction. Soulsby passed away in 1999. As a tribute, his funeral procession passed under the station's canopy on the way to the cemetery.

In 2003 Dragovich led volunteers in a major restoration effort that gave the station back its post–World War II color scheme. Today, looking like something out of a time machine, Soulsby's stands as a fitting tribute to Russell Soulsby and the glory days of Route 66.

HI CAFÉ-MOTEL AND RESTAURANT, STAUNTON
c. 1956

When the state of Illinois decided to change the path of Route 66 and send it south from Mt. Olive, following the route of I-55, Harold and Donna Hutchins had a problem. Their truck stop was on the same property upon which the new interstate exit ramps would be built. After a heated but futile battle with the state, they packed up and moved to Staunton, where they and partner Frank Intihar opened the Hi Café-Motel and Service Station.

This was a full-service tourist facility open 24 hours and featured a full garage and towing service. Their advertising slogan was "25 hour service on U.S. 66."

Prior to opening the business, a contest was held to name the new facility and stir up local publicity for the new café. A Staunton resident came up with the winning name by combining the first letters of the partners' last names, spelling out the word "Hi," as in "Hello."

The Hi Café became a popular eatery for locals and tourists alike. Summer was especially busy, recalls Donna Hutchins: "Bus loads of Chicago Cub fans on their way to and from St. Louis would always stop to eat."

The café closed in the 1980s, though the service station and motel continued on for a short while. Eventually, slowing business also forced the service station and motel to close. The 15 units that made up the motel now serve as storage units for Country View Mini Storage.

The Hi Café must have served some magnificent food. The street that runs perpendicular to Route 66, forming the corner that the café stood on, is named High Café Road. How many cafés get a street named after them—whether it's spelled correctly or not?

LUNA CAFÉ, MITCHELL
c. 1931

Irma Rafalala is given credit for building the two-story Luna Café in 1924, two years prior to the designation of Highway 66. The foundation was dug using old-fashioned mule power and a large scoop, recalls 82-year-old Mitchell resident Bud Eberhart. The restaurant/bar was located on the main floor, while bedrooms, often used by railroad workers, were located upstairs.

One of the oldest continuously run establishments on the Mother Road, the Luna Café has a colorful history that revolves around gangsters, upstairs brothels, and basement gambling. As co-owner Alan Young says, "It's hard to separate fact from fiction." One of the many rumors surrounding the Luna is that Al Capone and his gang regularly stopped at the café when traveling between St. Louis and Chicago. High-stakes gambling reportedly took place in the basement on a regular basis and probably was one of the reasons for Capone's alleged visits.

Another unconfirmed story is that the upstairs bedrooms were often used for prostitution. As the legend goes, when the neon cherry was lit on the vintage sign out front, the ladies were waiting and available upstairs. According to a current tenant who resides upstairs, "There was a bell in each room. They would ring from downstairs to let the girls know who was wanted." The wiring for the bells is rumored to still be there.

In its early days the Luna Café catered to an upscale crowd, and much of its well-to-do clientele came from nearby St. Louis. The 1931 photo shows a painted sign on the side of the building advertising Budweiser and the restaurant fare. Young assured me that the sign still exists, albeit hidden under the newer siding.

Today the Luna Café is a neighborhood tavern catering mostly to locals. However, when tourist travel on Historic Route 66 is at its peak during the summer months, people from all over the world can be seen sitting at tables eating sandwiches and at the bar drinking cold brews. The Luna Café's roadhouse charm oozes from every corner, and the myriad stories, whether fact or fiction, only add to it. It does not take much of an imagination to visualize Capone and his gang sitting at a back table, making plans for a future heist or counting the take from the gambling downstairs.

The Luna Café was inducted into the Illinois Route 66 Hall of Fame in June 2004 and is currently owned by Alan Young and Larry Wofford. It is a great spot to wet your whistle.

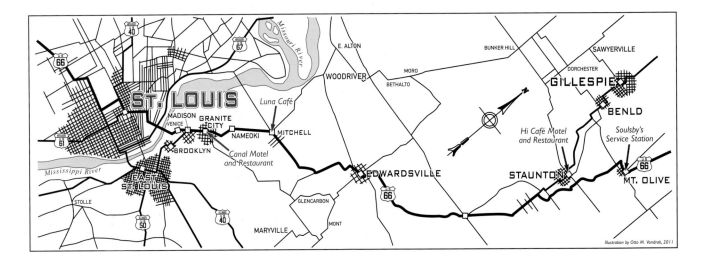

Illustration by Otto M. Vondrak, 2011

CANAL MOTEL AND RESTAURANT, GRANITE CITY
c. 1956

In 1936 when the Chain of Rocks Bridge was designated part of Route 66, a slew of motels sprang up along the Illinois approach to the bridge. This last portion of road prior to crossing the Mississippi was a logical location for overnight tourist facilities, given its proximity to St. Louis.

Navigating riverboats over this portion of the Mississippi was extremely hazardous and considered the most dangerous stretch of the entire river. In 1952, the Chain of Rocks Canal was completed, bypassing the infamous section and providing a safer channel for riverboat traffic. Even the mighty Mississippi was not immune to bypasses.

By the mid-1950s, the Illinois approach to the bridge not only turned into a "motel row," other tourist facilities including service stations, restaurants, and campgrounds became prevalent.

The Canal Motel sits on the south side of Route 66, now known as the Chain of Rocks Road. The Canal Motel's 12 units are configured in an L shape, with the office and restaurant fronting the property. The motel's amenities included tile baths, radiant heat, air conditioning, and TV in every room. A classic 1950s sign sat out front, tempting potential guests. Parts of the original sign still survive, including the frame and the very 1950s-looking portion advertising TV. The Canal Motel also bragged of being the nearest motel to the Chain of Rocks Bridge, making it the very last stop prior to reaching Missouri.

The stream of traffic traversing the toll bridge was constant and kept all of the businesses on motel row hopping. The Canal Motel and Restaurant enjoyed the parade of motorists for just over a decade. In 1967, a newer, safer, toll-free bridge was built just to the north. In 1968, citing the lack of tolls to help offset maintenance expenses, the city of Madison, Illinois, closed the bridge. Since the completion of the new bridge and the old bridge's closure, the motel and restaurant, now with an added bar, have scratched out a living by serving a few locals and travelers on Illinois Route 3. Local businesses have seen a slight increase in traffic recently with a surge of Route 66 tourists visiting the old Chain of Rocks Bridge.

Route 66 leaves the Illinois plains and crosses into Missouri at the Mississippi River. It then cuts diagonally across Missouri from St. Louis to the high plains southwest of Springfield. As it slices through the Ozarks, the highway follows approximately the same route as a stage line established by the U.S. government two decades before the Civil War. During the Civil War, this trail was an important military thoroughfare traveled by Union and Confederate troops alike. It was during that time the federal government installed a telegraph line along the road with stations at St. Louis, Rolla, Lebanon, Marshfield, and Springfield. The old stage line, previously known as the Kickapoo Trail, the Osage Trace, the Springfield Road, and the Military Road, thus became known as the Old Wire Road or Telegraph Road.

At Springfield, the road connected with what would become the Ozark Trail, headed west, and eventually terminated in Santa Rosa, New Mexico. The Ozark Trails Association established the Ozark Trail in 1915, and in August 1922, the newly formed Missouri State Highway Commission designated seven roads totaling about 1,500 miles as primary roads throughout the state, including State Route 14, the future U.S. Highway 66, laid on the former Old Wire Road. Work on the new highway progressed at a rapid pace, and on January 5, 1931, the last section of hard top was completed in Pulaski County, making Missouri the third of the eight Route 66 states to complete its paving through the entire state.

The new road helped Missouri flourish and become one of the most popular vacation destinations in the country. Rivers, lakes, and a wealth of forestland attracted sportsmen from around the nation. Travelers and vacationers alike found an abundance of motels, resorts, and lodges to choose from. These vacation destinations came in all sizes and shapes, but none were more recognizable than the stylized stone or "rocked" buildings that proliferated in the Ozarks.

Highly skilled "rock men," as they were called, carefully cut and placed slabs of colorful sandstone over the frames of buildings, creating the unique look often called "giraffe stone." At the height of its popularity in the late 1930s and into the late 1940s, scores of motels, cafés, gas stations, and homes were rocked in this style. Many examples of this style still exist along Route 66 in the Ozarks region, including the Wagon Wheel Motel featured in this chapter.

Also popular in Missouri were the abundant caves and caverns that became tourist attractions over the years. Signs painted on barns to advertise the caverns became common sights throughout the Midwest on Route 66. By the time travelers arrived in Missouri, they were almost literally brainwashed into stopping. As an incentive, one cave owner, Lester Dills of Meremec Caverns in Stanton, offered to paint farmers' barns for free if they allowed him to advertise on them. Not many refused his offer.

As in the other states through which Route 66 passes, the road underwent many alignment changes in Missouri. Roads were straightened to make them safer, towns were bypassed to create faster routes, and two-lane Route 66 was eventually upgraded to four lanes. With the passage of the Federal Highway Aid Act in 1956, Missouri began work almost immediately on its new Interstate. Lebanon holds the dubious honor of being the first town in Missouri to be bypassed by the new highway. By the dawn of the 1980s Interstate 44 had replaced most of Route 66 across the Show-Me State; a section of the highway at Devils Elbow was the last to be bypassed in 1981. Even so, many surviving stretches of old Route 66 still exist today and can be driven and explored. Many of the small towns and villages there still retain that old-time feel and vintage charm of the Mother Road's glory days. They're all just an Interstate exit away.

CHAIN OF ROCKS BRIDGE, ST. LOUIS
c. 1939

The $2.5 million Chain of Rocks Bridge spans the Mississippi River, connecting Granite City, Illinois, to North St. Louis, Missouri. This two-lane, mile-long bridge was built in 1929 and was one of six bridges in the St. Louis area to carry traffic over the Mississippi. The bridge was simultaneously built from both sides and was off by a mere 1/32 inch when the two sides met.

The Chain of Rocks Bridge is very unique in that it has a 22-degree bend halfway across its span. The original design was to be a straight shot across the river, but riverboat operators saw the plans and noted that the proximity of the bridge pilings to the water intake towers would make navigating the river at this point quite hazardous. The 22-degree bend was designed to expand the distance between foundation piers and alleviate possible navigation problems.

Originally, Route 66 traffic flowed over the MacArthur Bridge farther south, but in 1936 traffic was rerouted to the Chain of Rocks, allowing travelers to bypass the heavily congested downtown area. In 1939, federal regulations cut profits for private bridge owners and the Kingshighway Bridge Company was forced to sell. The city of

Madison, Illinois, bought the bridge for a mere $2.3 million. During World War II, with gasoline rationing in full swing, tolls were increased to 35 cents per car and 5 cents per each additional passenger. Madison lost the bridge in 1956 due to back taxes but quickly regained the title and holds it to this day. In 1958, tolls were dropped to 15 cents per automobile, and by 1966 Madison realized a net profit of $7 million from the bridge.

In 1967 a new, modern, and much wider bridge was built slightly to the north. Tolls were no longer collected to cross the old bridge and it became too expensive to maintain. The bridge was finally closed in 1968. Demolition plans were proposed in 1975, but by 1976, scrap-metal prices plummeted and tearing the bridge down was no longer profitable. Except for a scene filmed on the bridge for the movie *Escape from New York* with Kurt Russell, the bridge laid abandoned for 31 years. In 1999 the combined efforts of the Confluence Greenway Project and Trailnet funded its reopening as the world's longest pedestrian bridge.

CORAL COURT, MARLBOROUGH
c. 1942

John Carr built the fabled Coral Court just outside the city limits of St. Louis. The motel was painstakingly designed by architect Adolph L. Struebig, and construction began in summer 1941. By early 1942 the Coral Court greeted its first guest. Ten single-story units, with two rooms and two garages per unit, and an office structure were included. Almost immediately the Coral Court became a standout. The Streamline Moderne style, the elegant veneer of ceramic-glazed brick, and artful glass-block windows made it one-of-a-kind.

In 1946, 23 additional units designed by architect Harold T. Tyre were built using the same materials and varying only slightly from the original ten units. The new units featured triangular glass-block windows, but the overall look of the Coral Court remained. Another expansion took place in 1953 with the addition of three more ordinary-looking two-story units, also designed by Tyre, at the rear of the property. A swimming pool was added in the early 1960s.

Carr died in 1984, leaving the Coral Court to his wife, Jessie, and head housekeeper, Martha Shutt. Jessie and her second husband, Robert Williams, operated the business until August 20, 1993. Over time a lack of maintenance took its toll. During its later years the Coral Court began a swift decline, even garnering quite a racy reputation. The fact that you could park in a garage, close the garage

door, and enter the unit from inside the garage made the Coral Court a perfect rendezvous for star-crossed lovers. No guest vehicles were visible to jealous spouses driving through the grounds. As if that weren't enough, rooms could be rented in three-hour blocks.

Beginning in 1987 preservation groups fought to save the Coral Court from an untimely demise. The Coral Court was listed on the National Register of Historic Places on April 25, 1989. Sadly, the motel, except for one unit, was demolished in June 1995, and the new owners, Conrad Properties, began construction of the Oak Knoll Manor on the old Coral Court grounds.

Jessie (Carr) Williams passed away on October 15, 1996, a year after the razing of the Coral Court (Robert Williams had died on May 18, 1994).

The Coral Court's history is full of wonderful stories and anecdotes, which are covered in detail in *Tales from the Coral Court* by Shellee Graham. Luckily for fans of the Coral Court, the Missouri Museum of Transportation, with help from many volunteers, worked for weeks to disassemble a complete Coral Court building prior to the rest of the motel's demolition. The building was stored at the museum and rebuilt in all its glory, so that future generations will be able to view this work of art that just also happened to be a motel.

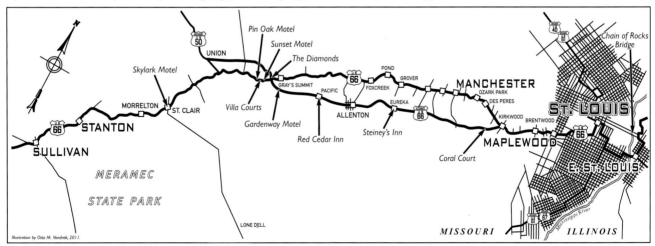

Illustration by Otto M. Vondrak, 2011.

MISSOURI

71

STEINY'S INN, EUREKA
c. 1947

Built in 1935, this restaurant/roadhouse was located on the south side of Route 66 near the east entrance of the 1931 bridge that spans the Meramec River. This bridge carried east- and westbound Route 66 traffic until the sheer volume of cars forced the construction of a second bridge that carried eastbound traffic, leaving the 1931 bridge to handle the westbound flow. By the early 1970s, the eastbound bridge was widened to handle traffic in both directions for the newly designated Interstate 44.

Originally known as the Bridgehead Inn, the roadhouse featured a bar, dance floor, and several overnight rooms located on the second floor. The Bridgehead Inn had a great reputation and was extremely popular with both travelers and locals.

On the west side of the bridge, Edward Steinberg operated a restaurant known as Steiny's. In 1946, a spectacular fire left Steiny's a charred ruin. That same year, Steinberg bought the Bridgehead Inn and renamed it Steiny's Inn.

William and Jeanette Klecka purchased the building in 1972 and reopened under the original Bridgehead Inn moniker, but 1980 saw another name change and the Bridgehead Inn became known as Galley West. The Galley West closed its doors in the mid-1980s.

At one point the Environmental Protection Agency occupied the former roadhouse building while working on a toxic waste disaster cleanup at nearby Times Beach. By 1997 the cleanup was complete and the property was turned over to the Missouri Department of Natural Resources. The plan was to develop the restored land into a state park with a Route 66 theme. In September 1999 the much anticipated Route 66 State Park was opened to the public. The former Steiny's Inn serves as the park visitor center and appears much the same as it did during its days as a popular roadhouse. As of this writing the bridge at the park is permanently closed.

RED CEDAR INN, PACIFIC
c. 1941

Brothers Bill and James Smith built the Red Cedar Inn in 1934 out of red cedar logs, which were cut from the family farm in nearby Villa Ridge and hauled to the construction site on a Ford Model AA truck. The structure's logs were all hewn with an ax, while the foundation was dug using mule power.

Soon after the inn's opening, sometime in 1935, a barroom was added to the facility. During the early years the inn offered gasoline service from two pumps out front. The sale of gasoline was eventually halted, and all efforts were focused on the restaurant business. In 1935, acting as manager of operations, James Smith II hired 19-year-old Katherine Brinkman to wait tables. It was the hiring of his life—the two soon fell in love and were married in 1940. Katherine and James II eventually purchased the business from his father in 1944.

Alongside son James III and daughter Ginger, the couple ran the business until James II retired in 1972. In 1987 Ginger and her father reopened the Red Cedar Inn with a little help from Katherine, who continued to bake the restaurant's delicious brownies.

The Red Cedar Inn was a classic example of the family-run businesses that proliferated on the highway during the glory days of Route 66. These businesses were slapped together with guts and hard work. Some continue to operate today, requiring even harder work to survive. Like the Red Cedar Inn, many have been handed down from generation to generation. Officially listed on the National Register of Historic Places on June 22, 2003, the Red Cedar Inn unfortunately ceased operation in 2005 and was up for sale at the time of this book's publication.

GARDENWAY MOTEL, GRAY SUMMIT
c. 1950

On the 30-mile stretch of Highway 66 between St. Louis and the Missouri Botanical Garden Arboretum at Gray Summit, the roadside was once lined with thousands of decorative shrubs, lush trees, and native flowers. The National Park Service and the Missouri State Highway Commission, in conjunction with the Missouri Botanical Garden, combined forces to create this remarkable landscaping and preserve the natural indigenous plant life of Missouri for future generations. Billed as the Henry Shaw Gardenway, in honor of the man who founded the Missouri Botanical Garden back in 1858, the project was completed in 1937.

In 1945 Louis B. Eckelkamp built his Colonial-style motel at the western edge of the Gardenway, near his home and adjacent to the Missouri Botanical Garden Arboretum. By 1954 the Gardenway Motel featured "Twenty-five Modern Cabins with Tile Baths." The motel eventually grew to also include 41 guest rooms.

The beautiful Streamline Moderne Gardenway sign beckoning motorists near the edge of the road sits in stark contrast to the motel's sprawling American Colonial architecture. When lit up, this sign stands out as the ultimate in classic Route 66 motel signage. Today the motel still waits patiently to serve vacationers and business travelers. The neon sign, on the other hand, waits to be brought back to life, longing for the flick of the switch that will once again breathe life into its colorful neon glass.

THE DIAMONDS, VILLA RIDGE
c. 1948

Location, location, location—the key to success for any restaurant. At the junction of Routes 50, 66, and 100, The Diamonds utilized all three. Spencer Groff knew he had an envious location when he opened the first Diamonds on July 3, 1927. As word spread the restaurant quickly became known from coast to coast for fine food and courteous service. In 1948 a spectacular fire destroyed the original Diamonds and traffic was brought to a halt in both directions on Route 66 for hours as smoke covered the road. Groff and business partner Louis Eckelkamp (who also owned the nearby Gardenway Motel) rebuilt the Diamonds in an ultramodern streamlined style alongside 25 cottages and a swimming pool. In 1967 Interstate 44 bypassed the area and The Diamonds and its facilities were moved to new buildings farther east near the I-44 access ramp at Gray Summit. Interstate construction also forced the closure of the Tri-County Truck Stop 20 miles west in Sullivan. Owners Arla and Roscoe Reed in 1971 chose the abandoned Diamonds building to house the new Tri-County Truck Stop. Ironically, the relocated Diamonds Restaurant, once billed as the "World's Largest Roadside Restaurant," is now closed and abandoned, while the Tri-County Truck Stop remains open on the site of the second Diamonds, and continues to serve hungry truckers and tourists traveling I-44 and Route 66.

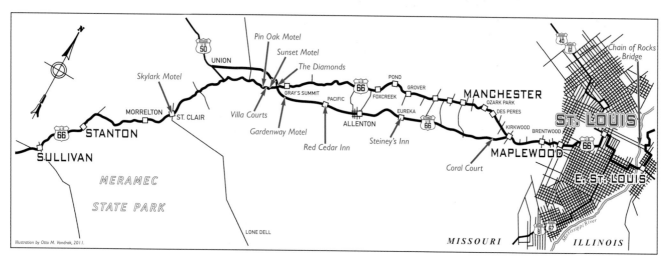

SUNSET MOTEL, VILLA RIDGE
c. 1942

Built in the early 1940s, the 12-unit Sunset Motel stands out as one of the more distinctive motels of the era. Located 38 miles west of St. Louis, the Sunset was built of beige brick and laid out in a V shape in which the exterior center of the V served as a community area equipped with ice and soda machines. One of the more unusual aspects of this motel is the fact that it was built with two entrances per unit: one entrance in front of each unit overlooking a sprawling, beautifully landscaped lawn area, and the other providing entrance from the parking lot and driveway behind the structure.

Today the motel stands much as it did when it was built over 60 years ago. The original eye-catching signage also remains intact and over the years has evolved into a Route 66 must-see photo op. "Twelve Units, Twelve Baths, Panel Ray Heat, Beautyrest Mattresses and Quiet" was the advertising copy that attracted weary motorists to the Sunset. The interstate bypass in 1967 added an exclamation point to the word "Quiet," and the Sunset Motel now sits empty and silent, fading in the golden twilight.

VILLA COURTS, VILLA RIDGE
c. 1947

Villa Courts opened in 1928, just a few years after Highway 66 began carrying auto traffic from Chicago to Los Angeles. A man named Stropman built an auto camp on the property and appropriately dubbed it Stropman's Camp. This early auto camp was primitive, but not as primitive as most auto camps were in the early days of cross-country auto travel. Stropman's offered more than a just a safe place to park your car for the night.

The building you see behind the pumps served as Stropman's original office and grocery store. The grocery, used both by travelers and locals, carried everything an auto traveler might require for the night as well as necessities for the next day's journey. The community restrooms gave travelers a chance to freshen up prior to setting off the next morning.

Stropman's Camp was located only 2 miles west of the famous Diamonds restaurant and cabins. If the Diamonds was full or you wanted the peace and quiet of a smaller facility, Stropman's was your choice. The Diamonds had a reputation for fine food; many travelers staying at Stropman's would make the short 2-mile trip and have their meals there.

No one seems to know when Stropman's ownership ended and the name changed to Villa Courts. The Guffeys purchased the business around 1976 and changed the name of the grocery from Villa Courts Grocery to Villa Ridge Foods. By this time, the cabins were no longer used for overnight stays but rented by the month. In the early 1990s, the cabins were closed altogether and are now utilized for storage.

Villa Ridge Foods, or "Guffey's" as the locals know it, remains an integral part of the local landscape and the lives of Villa Ridge residents. Steve Guffey told me several of their older and most loyal customers have been coming to the store since it was known as Stropman's. Loyal indeed.

PIN OAK MOTEL - RT. 1, VILLA RIDGE, MO.

PIN OAK MOTEL, VILLA RIDGE
c. 1953

The Pin Oak Motel was built around 1940 some 40 miles west of St. Louis and was named for the beautiful pin oak trees that dominate the local landscape. The Pin Oak was originally laid out with two sets of two buildings. The buildings were joined by common carports and faced each other across a courtyard. Originally just eight units were available, but by the early 1950s more units had been added and the carports were enclosed. Eventually the room count grew to 28.

A member of the American Motor Hotel Association, the Pin Oak was billed as "a better court for better people" and was advertised as having "clean, ultra-modern units." In the early 1960s, free air conditioning, free TV, and new carpets were added to the list of amenities. In 1967, however, Interstate 44 bypassed the area and, like so many other motels, the Pin Oak fell on hard times. Eventually converted into a self-storage facility, the old Pin Oak Motel stands as a relic to the glory days of Route 66, safely storing memories of its past alongside family treasures within its aging walls.

ROCK HAVEN CABINS, ST. JAMES
c. 1940

The Rock Haven is a classic example of a 1920s and early-1930s motor court. These overnight rest stops provided simple, modest accommodations for tourists as well as traveling businessmen. Opened shortly after Highway 66 was designated a U.S. highway, the Rock Haven offered six small "modern" cabins built of native sandstone slabs known as giraffe rock. This rock was a common sight in the region and was used to build everything from homes and motels to filling stations and restaurants. Indoor plumbing was not typical of early motor courts and was, in fact, considered a luxury. The Rock Haven, like many original auto courts of the day, provided a community washhouse with hot and cold running water for showers.

In 1950 Frank and Ruth Waring purchased the Rock Haven and that summer added a wooden double cabin, a restaurant, and a new filling station that sold Standard Oil gasoline. In 1954 the Warings sold the business to Rudy Gilder, who operated the Rock Haven until the interstate bypassed it in the late 1960s. Converted to a nightclub and tavern in the 1970s, the restaurant building, although somewhat altered, is today a private residence. In 1988 all but one of the cabins were razed, leaving a small but tantalizing glimpse into the past of American auto travel and the halcyon days of Highway 66.

WAGON WHEEL MOTEL, CUBA
c. 1934

The Wagon Wheel Motel on the eastern end of Cuba is one of the most recognizable landmarks on Route 66. Originally known as the Wagon Wheel Cabin Court, it was built by Robert and Margaret Martin, with local stonemason Leo Friescenhan hired as designer and construction supervisor. Originally a nine-room motel, Ozark Stone and brick trim on the windows and porches give it the classic "rocked" look that was popular in the region. The Wagon Wheel once boasted "All modern steam heated, fireproof cottages," as was printed on the back of this postcard. In the 1930s rooms rented for $1.50 and up per night. By 1946 the motel had expanded to 14 units, a number that grew to 18 when the garages were enclosed and converted. A service station and 24-hour café were also on the property, but were owned independently of the motel.

When I-44 bypassed the area in the late 1960s the motel's future looked bleak, but the Wagon Wheel managed to hang on. The motel has had several owners during its lifetime (one of them, a Mr. Mathis, designed the very recognizable neon sign), but Harold and Pauline Armstrong, owners for more than 40 years, attribute continued success to clean, quiet rooms at a great price. Venerable longtime caretaker Roy Mudd, who has been tending to the property for forty years, is as much a part of the classic motel as the neon sign and the Ozark stone.

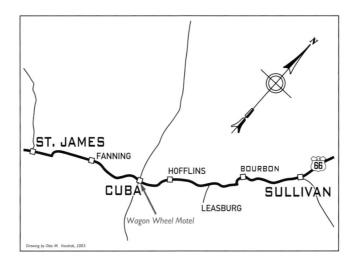

Drawing by Otto M. Vondrak, 2003.

MULE TRADING POST, ROLLA
c. 1970

In 1946, Frank Ebling opened a restaurant and gift shop along Route 66 in Pacific, Missouri. He quickly tired of the restaurant business when he realized he was making more money selling souvenir items than hot lunches. In the finest tradition of Route 66 entrepreneurship, he quickly ceased the restaurant operation and filled the store with trinkets and souvenirs. For more than a decade the business flourished and grew to become one of the largest outlets in the Ozarks. In 1957, the Mule Trading Post moved to a new location just east of Rolla as a result of the interstate bypassing Pacific.

Former Ozark souvenir salesman Herb Baden purchased the business from Ebling in 1966. Tiring of the traveling salesman grind, Baden yearned to settle down and spend more time with his family. In 1962 he had taken a job managing a Stuckey's Pecan Shop, but when the Mule Trading Post came up for sale he jumped at the opportunity. The Mule Trading Post was one of his largest accounts during his years as a salesman, so he knew business was good. It was the perfect fit.

During his tenure as owner, the business continued to grow. Realizing advertising was key to success, he plastered the region with blue and yellow billboards featuring the iconic cartoon-like mule-head logo, making the already popular Mule Trading Post a Missouri legend.

In March 1995, Baden had his fill of the business and was ready to retire. He turned over the reins to Jack and Janiece Williams. They sold the business in 2004 to Carl and Zelma Smith who continue to nurture the popular Mule Trading Post. Two interstate bypasses, the demise of Route 66, and 60-plus years have passed since Frank Ebling brought the Mule Trading Post to life. Like its namesake, the trading post remains steadfast and stubborn and refuses to fade away. Let's hope it's kickin' for years to come.

SCHUMAN'S TOURIST CITY, ROLLA
c. 1939

R. E. Schuman opened his "tourist city" in 1928, hoping to capitalize on the newly designated Highway 66 that ran through town. According to a quote from the *Rolla Herald* on June 27, 1929, "Seventeen clean comfortable cottages, ideally suited at the north city limits of Rolla, will cause thousands of tourists to stop in our city each season. It is a general comment of tourists that the Schuman Cottages are the nicest and cleanest along the highways."

Originally known as Schuman's Cottage City, then as Schuman's Tourist City, the business was known as Schuman's Motor Inn in the 1950s and 1960s. From the day the first cottages were completed in 1928, Schuman constantly made improvements to the guest units and to the grounds, adding conveniences such as covered parking, steam heat, radios, and telephones. By the late 1930s, Schuman's Tourist City also included a service station, café, and a two-story hotel with accommodations for 100 guests. The hotel was billed as offering "all the facilities of a fine city hotel combined with the conveniences of an ultra modern motor court."

In 1931 an armed gunman held up Schuman's, leading the owners to hire a watchman to patrol the grounds at night. The patrolman carried a watch clock that he punched at designated stations throughout the grounds, covering "all parts of the court and all floors of the hotel," as the back of a period postcard states.

Schuman became a prominent businessman in the Rolla area and owned several other businesses, including the Central Missouri Hatchery that turned out thousands of baby chicks a week, and a commercial flower garden located adjacent to the motel. Surviving well into the 1960s as Schuman's Motor Inn, the former Tourist City eventually closed. Today its past is a distant, fading memory for thousands of tourists who made Schuman's a unique "city" unto itself as they made their way to untold destinations along Route 66.

PARTIAL VIEW, SCHUMAN'S TOURIST CITY, ROLLA, MO.

ROLLA
c. 1940s

Rolla originated in 1855 when a group of contractors engaged in construction of the St. Louis, San Francisco Railway (aka "the Frisco") selected the area for supply warehouses and a railway office. According to legend, a local resident named George Coopedge, who was homesick for his native North Carolina, suggested the name Raleigh. The name was accepted and the decision was made to spell it exactly the way George pronounced it. The concrete paving of two-lane Route 66 through Missouri was completed in 1931 and was greeted by the citizens of Rolla with a huge public celebration that included a grand parade. There was cause for a celebration as the new and improved roadway meant increased traffic through town, which resulted in a much-needed boost for business at the local cafés, service stations, and motels that lined the town's main street. A couple of miles west of town in 1925, on the site of an old pioneer cabin, was built the Old Homestead, which today stands as one of the country's first truck stops.

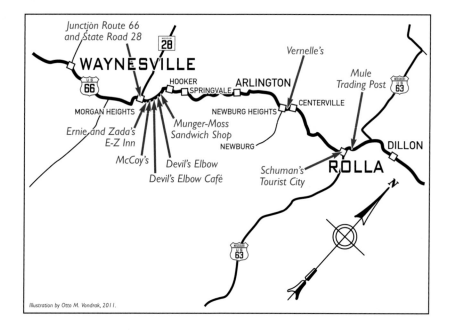

Illustration by Otto M. Vondrak, 2011.

DEVILS ELBOW
c. 1939

Devils Elbow is a quiet, picturesque village on the Big Piney River about 20 miles west of Rolla. Listed as one of Missouri's top scenic spots, this Ozarks town was named by lumberjacks who floated logs down to this treacherous portion of the river. The logs would often jam at the bend and cause long delays, leading the rafters to comment that the river at this point had a "devil of an elbow."

A block east of the bridge leading into Devils Elbow sits the Elbow Inn (originally Munger-Moss Sandwich Shop). Across the bridge is the site of the old Devils Elbow Café and the Conoco station built by Dwight Rench in 1932. The café and station were at one time affiliated with the nearby Cedar Lodge, 10 cabins boasting private cooking facilities. The café housed the local post office from 1931 to 1941, and in later years was transformed into a tavern called The Hideaway, which burned to the ground in the late 1950s. A block from the café was McCoy's Store and Camp, an old-fashioned general store built by Charles McCoy in 1941. In addition to selling fishing tackle and sporting goods, McCoy's rented boats for use on the Big Piney, as well as six small sleeping rooms upstairs; the

Devils Elbow Cafe
Devils Elbow, Mo.

owners lived in a four-bedroom apartment downstairs behind the store. In 1948 seven small cabins were added, but McCoy's closed in 1954 and was turned into an apartment building.

That year, McCoy's son-in-law, Atholl "Jiggs" Miller, and his wife Dorothy built Millers Market, and sold camping essentials, dry goods, and gasoline. Jiggs was the postmaster until 1982 when he sold the market to Terry and Marilyn Allman, who operated the store as Allman's Market until October 2001, when the property was sold to Phil Sheldon, who changed the name to Sheldon's Market. Sheldon had managed The Hideaway for a year before entering the army in

1942. About a mile west of downtown sat Ernie and Zada's Inn, also known as the E-Z Inn. Built in the late 1930s it consisted of a Sinclair station, restaurant, and cabins and had a wild reputation as a honky-tonk. It closed after only a few years of operation, according to Sheldon. The building that once served as the gas station and restaurant is now a private residence.

In 1943 Route 66 bypassed the town was to accommodate heavy military traffic from nearby Fort Leonard Wood, and in the early 1980s Interstate 44 completely left Devils Elbow behind.

DANCING, FISHING, HUNTING, SHADY TRAILER CAMP, DINNERS, LUNCHES, BEER MODERN CABINS WITH IN-SPR. MATTRESS

E161 ERNIE & ZADA'S INN HI-WAY 66 1 MILE WEST OF DEVIL'S ELBOW, MO. Schuster Studio Hermann, Mo.

"McCOY'S"
AT DEVIL'S ELBOW, MO.

ERNIE & ZADA'S E-Z INN, DEVILS ELBOW
c. 1939

West of "downtown" Devils Elbow sits the remains of Ernie & Zada's E-Z Inn. Acknowledging a downtown in Devils Elbow is a bit misleading considering its size, but the inn is approximately a mile west of Sheldon's Market and what probably can be considered downtown Devils Elbow.

The inn was built in the late 1930s and, according to the locals, quickly developed a reputation for being a wild beer-brawling, jukebox honky tonk. During the inn's heyday there existed a trailer camp, several "modern cabins with inner spring mattresses," a restaurant, and a Sinclair service station. The restaurant featured lunches in the afternoon and dinner and dancing in the evening.

In this region of Missouri, hunting and fishing was and is a major tourist draw. The E-Z Inn catered to outdoorsmen and soon became a popular stop for tourists looking to hunt down that large trophy deer or net that record-breaking bass in the Big Piney. Unfortunately, serving Falstaff and Blatz beer to hunters and fisherman was not enough to keep the inn's doors open. Ernie & Zada's E-Z Inn closed just a few years after opening. "Lack of business and hard times" was the reason, according to Phil Sheldon, owner of Sheldon's Market. The onetime gas station and restaurant still stands, as do several of the tourist cabins. The building that once housed the restaurant and gas station now serves as a private residence.

JUNCTION HIGHWAY 66 AND STATE ROAD 28, MORGAN HEIGHTS
c. 1929

When Highway 66 was in its infancy, its path was carved mostly out of existing state and county dirt roads. This is quite apparent in this early photo showing the original dirt Highway 66 joining with dirt State Road 28. Early highway shields, gas stations, and bus stops are also represented in this photo hearkening back to a time when cross-country auto and bus travel were still new. It is noteworthy to point out that this bus stop was serviced by Pickwick Lines, which later merged with Northland Transportation to form Greyhound Bus Line in 1930. Morgan Heights Hotel and Café once stood across from the gas station and bus stop.

The dirt 66 in the photo was paved by the early 1930s. During World War II, the massive increase in military traffic from nearby Ft. Leonard Wood deemed it necessary to build a new four-lane alignment bypassing the original path of Highway 66 and the tourist facilities in Morgan Heights. This new alignment was the first four-lane stretch of 66 in Missouri.

In 1981, the interstate came bullying through and devastated both the original and newer alignments of Route 66, leaving several short sections and unusable dead ends in its path. The devastation brought by the interstate is evident in the modern photo. As you follow Highway 28 up in the modern photo, the junction with Route 66 as seen in the vintage photo is situated on the right. The Highway 66 in the vintage photo, going off to the right and down, still exists as a dead-end section cut off by the interstate on one end and barricaded with dirt on the other.

Take a long and careful look at the vintage photo and remember you are looking at a state-of-the-art tourist facility of its day.

WAYNESVILLE
c. 1940s

Waynesville was established in 1833 as a simple trading post for settlers and trappers on the Roubidoux River, and was named for General "Mad" Anthony Wayne, a hero of the Revolutionary War. The stretch of Route 66 in this area can be traced back to the early 1800s when an overland trail was established between St. Louis and Springfield. The trail's various names spell out its history: Kickapoo Trail, the Osage Trace, Old Wire Road, Old Springfield Road, Highway 14, and eventually U.S Highway 66.

Many buildings in Waynesville survive from the 1920s and 1930s, including the former Bell Hotel (now Waynesville Memorial Chapel) built by Robert Bell. In anticipation of the coming tourist trade from the new Highway 66, Bell expanded his home in 1925 and turned it

into the Bell Hotel. It operated until 1937 under the slogan "Every Facility for the Traveler's Pleasure – Old Southern Hospitality." Through the hard times of the 1920s and 1930s Waynesville's status as the seat of Pulaski County, combined with the ever-increasing tourist travel on Route 66, kept the town alive. In 1941 the construction of nearby Fort Leonard Wood brought thousands of military and construction workers to the area, and as World War II unfolded Waynesville became the primary place of recreation for men and women stationed on the base. Since then, Waynesville has had its share of ups and downs, good times and bad, but the friendliness and small-town ways have remained constant.

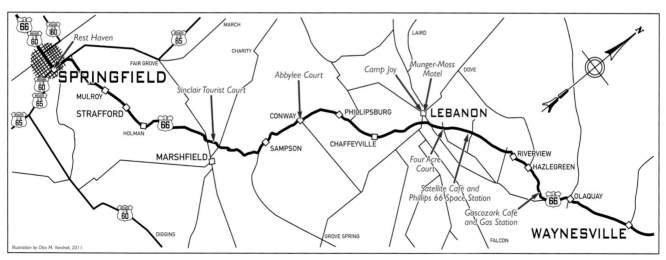

Illustration by Otto M. Vondrak, 2011.

GASCOZARK CAFÉ
AND GAS STATION, GASCOZARK
c. 1939

In 1931, Frank A. Jones built the Gascozark Café and Gas Station, which he owned and operated along with a popular tourist and fishing resort on the nearby Gasconade River. Jones, who originally settled in the area in the 1920s, in fact coined the town name "Gascozark" as a combination of *Gasconade* and Ozark. The former refers to the Gascony region of France that lent its name to the nearby river; the latter is a distortion of the French *Aux Arc*. *Aux* (sounds like "oh") means "to" and *arc* is short for one of the region's native tribes. "Ozark," hence, literally means "to the Arkansas."

As tourist traffic on Route 66 steadily increased, so did business at the café and Jones soon made additions to the main building. In the mid-1930s Rudy and Clara Schuermann bought and took over the business. In 1939 the Schuermanns hired a Mr. Lillard, a "rock man," who added the large Ozark stones around the front and sides to alleviate the patchy look of the main building and its add-ons. In the 1940s the Gascozark Café and Gas Station became a regular stop on the Greyhound bus line, providing a substantial boost in business. In the 1950s another transformation to the café took place when it became a local hot spot known as the Spinning Wheel Tavern. In later years the building served as a private residence but as of this writing it sits vacant.

SATELLITE CAFÉ AND PHILLIPS 66 SPACE STATION, LEBANON
c. 1955

The Satellite Café and Space Station were located 4 miles east of Lebanon on a beautiful wooded stretch of Route 66. Although the facility included both a café and gas station, they were owned and operated separately. Norma and Loren Alloway owned the café, and the Phillips 66 Space Station was owned by LeRoy Hawkins. Locals referred to this popular roadside stop as simply "the Space Station."

The Satellite Café was a very popular tourist stop and greatly supported by locals. Norma did the cooking and was well-known for her fried chicken, homemade pies, and oatmeal cake. As a convenience to travelers, a picnic area including tables was located at the rear of the café. During the café's heyday, a neon sign in the form of a rocket stood on the roof to attract motorists.

The Phillips 66 Space Station sported a modern-looking, 20-foot rocket alongside the road, beckoning customers to check their oil and fill up on gas.

Although beautiful, this stretch of Route 66 was at one time one of the most dangerous. While the interstate in this area was under development, two-lane Route 66 became the eastbound lanes for I-44 until the early 1970s when construction on I-44 was complete. This caused many an accident as locals, accustomed to driving both directions on this stretch of Route 66, would head west to Lebanon, sometimes meeting eastbound traffic head-on with horrific results.

After the interstate was completed, both the Space Station and the Satellite Café eventually closed. The mostly empty café-turned-storage shed burned in 1999 leaving only a worn, deteriorating sign to mark its location; a canopy that once provided shade to customers marks the Phillips 66 station. Today the canopy continues to provide a shady rest spot, albeit for herds of cows that lazily graze on the tall grass where the Satellite Café once stood.

4 ACRE COURT, LEBANON
c. 1939

Ray Coleman and Blackie Walters built the 4 Acre Court in 1939 in the hopes of cashing in on the ever-increasing flow of traffic heading down Highway 66. To attract vacationing families, they built individual cabins with a fireplace in each. The cabins were "rocked" using the giraffe-stone exterior that was so popular in this region of the Ozarks during the 1930s and 1940s. For the more adventurous travelers, a campground was located to the west of the main building. This campground was eventually turned into a children's playground. A two-story building out front served as the owners' residence and office and at one time also housed a gas station and convenience store.

Today the one- and two-room cottages comprise an apartment complex called Village Oaks. In 2003 one of the cottages was destroyed by fire, but luckily none of the other remaining units were damaged.

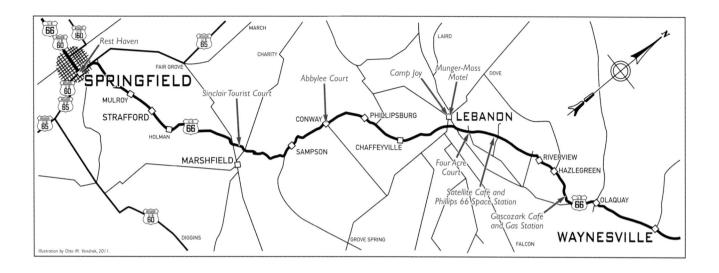

Illustration by Otto M. Vondrak, 2011.

MUNGER MOSS MOTEL, LEBANON
c. 1950s

Jesse and Pete Hudson, onetime owners of the Munger Moss Sandwich Shop in Devils Elbow, relocated in Lebanon after Devils Elbow was bypassed. Property in Lebanon was purchased in 1945 and the Munger Moss Motor Court was built in 1946 and originally consisted of seven buildings housing two units each and a garage. Rooms rented for $3 a night. Eleven more buildings were eventually added along the semicircular driveway, adding 44 new rooms. As tourist business increased during the postwar era so did demand for more rooms. As with many motels of the era, the attached garages were converted into rooms. Television came to the area in the early 1950s and tacked an extra 50 cents to the room rate. A swimming pool, new office, and sign were added in the late 1950s; all three are still in use today.

Bob and Ramona Lehman bought the motel in 1971 and have been its caretakers ever since. Ramona has gloriously decorated a few of the rooms with Route 66 themes: Room 18 is the famous Coral Court Room, a must see for Route 66 enthusiasts. Room 66 is, of course, the Munger Moss Historic Room, filled with old photos and memorabilia. Illinois, Kansas, Oklahoma, and Missouri all have rooms decorated in their honor, and the motel is one of the cleanest and well kept along all of Route 66.

CAMP JOY, LEBANON
c. 1930

Leaving Nebraska City, Nebraska, behind, Ernis and Lois Spears, accompanied by Ernis' parents, traveled back and forth on the new U.S. Highway 66 during the late 1920s in search of the perfect spot for a new tourist camp. Upon arriving in each town the two couples surveyed the area for possibilities, often spending days in one spot, counting passing cars. They found what they were looking for in Lebanon. Camp Joy, which began with 50-cents-a-night tent rentals, was so successful that Ernis and his father Charles built cabins. Eventually, attached carports were converted to drive-in garages and then to more rooms. As tourist travel increased so did tourist demands, and indoor plumbing in each cabin replaced a communal bathhouse.

By the end of 1935 Camp Joy featured 24 cabins that rented for $1.25 to $4, depending on the number of rooms. A gas station and café were added but were eventually moved to accommodate even more cabins. A drive-through archway read "Camp Joy" on the entrance side and "Teach your baby to say Camp Joy" on the exit side. According to Joy Spears Fishel, Ernis and Lois' daughter, customers in the early days seemed more like friends than customers: "In the evenings after supper, people would get out and visit. TV made a big difference. TV and air conditioning. After those came in, people didn't want to get together anymore." The Spears owned and operated the property until 1971. The few cabins still standing are now rented on a monthly basis.

ABBYLEE COURT, CONWAY
c. 1942

Thirty-two miles east of Springfield, Missouri, nestled among the wooded, rolling hills of the Missouri Ozarks, sits the remains of the onetime Abbylee Court. Built by a Mr. Haymes in the 1920s, the scenic auto court consisted of eight spacious, individual cabins situated around a semicircular, gravel-filled driveway. Billed as the Abbylee Court "Among the Trees," this auto court was one of the more secluded rest stops along all of Highway 66.

Considered large by the standards of the day, these cabins offered tourists more than ample room to stretch out and relax. Each was built with a private attached garage. These are still in use today. A café featuring "Meals and Sandwiches" was conveniently set in the center of the semicircle and was known throughout the area for having simple but good food. Sunday brunch was especially popular among the locals. This central structure also housed the rental office.

In 1950, the café building and one of the cabins fell victim to a blazing fire. Much to the disappointment of loyal customers, the popular eating establishment was never rebuilt.

Alan Jackson from nearby Niangua purchased the Abbylee around 2000 and proceeded to renovate the property. The Abbylee no longer serves the traveling public but operates as a monthly rental property. Today, tired and weary travelers may not be able to take advantage of the private setting, but current residents can still sit back after a hard day's work and relax "Among the Trees."

LOG CITY CAMP
14½ MILES EAST OF CARTHAGE M
ON HIGHWAY 66

DINING ROOM
LOG CITY CAMP

BLAKE
Photo

no1
COTTAGE AT LOG CITY CAMP
ON HIGHWAY 66
14½ MILES EAST OF
CARTHAGE MO.

KEL-LAKE MOTEL, CARTHAGE
c. 1954

The Kel-Lake Motel is located on the eastern edge of Carthage and sits across from Kellogg Lake. The motel was built on the southwest corner of the newer eastern approach to Carthage and the older Route 66 (now County Road V), bypassing the older route that snaked its way through Kellogg Lake Park then into Carthage proper. This newer approach was completed in the early 1950s.

The motel catered to travelers as well as vacationing fishermen taking advantage of the motel's proximity to Kellogg Lake. The Kel-Lake Motel consisted of eight guest units set up in a single line with parking in front of each unit. The motel was AAA recommended and offered tile baths, air conditioning, steam heat, and 7-foot beds.

The motel was purchased in May 2007 by Tom and Judy Wright. The previous owner, Gene Jackson, operated the motel for about 10 years. Judy, a former employee of Jackson's, managed the Kel-Lake Motel for a little over three years before she and her husband decided to purchase the property and go into the motel business.

Judy says they plan on "restoring and updating the eight rooms one by one" and are currently working on the first room. The Wrights also plan to build four cabins out back to serve as weekly rentals. The motel is mostly booked with weekly and monthly rentals but "a few rooms are always saved for overnight guests" says Judy.

Thankfully, Tom and Judy have also taken steps to fully restore the classic 1950s sign out front and hope to light up the sky with new paint and neon shortly.

By the late 1960s, Interstate 44 was completed south of town and Route 66 found itself playing second fiddle to the super slab. Happily, Carthage was and is much more than just a Route 66 town—and it survived the bypass well. Carthage has much to offer not only the Route 66 historian but also anyone interested in a perspective on life in the United States from pre–Civil War through the turn of the twentieth century. Spend some time in Carthage. You will not be sorry.

BOOTS COURT, CARTHAGE
c. 1949

Situated at the corner of Route 66 and Highway 71 at the so-called "Crossroads of America" sits the Boots Motel, one of the most recognizable landmarks on all of Route 66. Built by Arthur Boots in 1939, the distinctly streamline moderne motel began with four units of two rooms each. Classic pink and green neon follow the graceful lines of the motel, and a covered driveway allows guests to park next to their rooms. A Mobil station that once sat out front was eliminated to make space for more rooms. Early advertising boasted of "A radio in every room," and Clark Gable is rumored to have stayed in Room 6 and signed the guest book, "Clark Gable and Party."

In 1942 Ples Nelly bought the Boots Motel and added five rooms at the rear of the complex. In 1948, Ruben and Rachel Asplin bought the property, longing to leave the cold winters of Minnesota behind. After Ruben's death, Rachel continued to run the motel until her death in 1991 at the age of 91. Current owner John Ferguson rents rooms on a weekly basis only, but still turns on the classic neon every night. The motel's listing on the National Register of Historic Places would be a shoo-in if not for the nonoriginal pitched roof that was added in later years. At the time of this writing Ferguson was hoping for a buyer to restore the Boots to its former glory.

JUNCTION 66 AND 71, CARTHAGE, MO.

BOOTS DRIVE-IN, CARTHAGE
c. 1946

Seven years after building the iconic Boots Court, Arthur G. Boots expanded his enterprise and built the Boots Drive-In. Boots gave travelers a comfortable place to spend the night, and the addition of the drive-in opposite the court on the east side of Route 66 offered a good place to eat. One could hardly stay at the motel without being tempted by the mouth-watering aroma of sizzling chicken and burgers drifting from across the road. Not only did the two businesses share the same sexy, geometrically rounded corners, but the same classic pink and green neon that lit up Boots Court on a nightly basis also adorned the exterior of Boots Drive-In.

Boots Court and Boots Drive-In were tactically located at one of the many busy intersections along Route 66 that folks coined the "Crossroads of America." It is right here that Highway 66 running from Chicago to Los Angeles and Highway 71 from New Orleans to Canada intersected. The intersection prompted such hoopla that a national radio program was broadcast from the drive-in. "Breakfast at the Crossroads" sent its radio waves directly from the drive-in on a daily basis from 8:00 to 8:30 a.m. and was heard by millions. Throughout the 1950s, tourist traffic through the "Crossroads of America" was brisk and business was just as good.

Eventually Boots Drive-In became known as Boots Drive-In and Gift Shop when novelty items and souvenirs were added to the tasty drive-in fare. When the interstate reared its ugly head, business began to take a turn for the worse and even the addition of the gift shop could not prevent the inevitable. Boots Drive-In sold its last burger and chicken basket in 1970. The building survives today as the Great Plains Federal Credit Union.

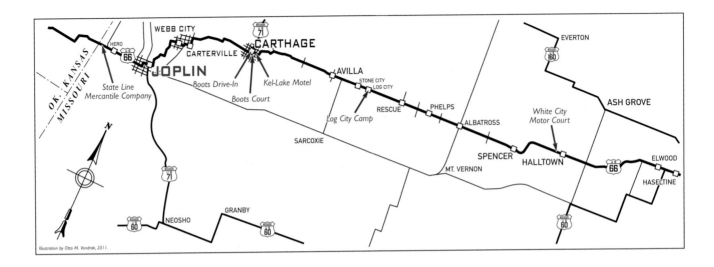

Illustration by Otto M. Vondrak, 2011.

JOPLIN
c. 1940s

Joplin holds the honor of being one of the 14 Route 66 cities forever immortalized in Bobby Troup's legendary hit song "Route 66." Located on the Ozark Plateau in the southwest corner of Missouri, just 200 miles from the geographical center of the country, Joplin was established in 1848 and was once known as the lead and zinc mining capital of the world. It was named for Reverend Harris G. Joplin, who founded the first Methodist Church in Jasper County in 1840. Because of its central location, Joplin became a major shipping point for many of the country's largest trucking companies.

Excessive mining has created many problems for the city, including a number of street cave-ins caused by the numerous abandoned mine tunnels under the city. As a result, Route 66 saw many alignment changes in Joplin over the years, including a City 66, Alternate 66, and a Bypass 66.

From 1979 to the route's demise in 1985, the Joplin area was designated the easternmost terminus of Route 66. During the glory days of the Mother Road, Main Street in downtown Joplin was a bustling and thriving entity lined with huge department stores, no less than 20 hotels, banks, eight movie houses, and every type of shop imaginable. Back during Joplin's rowdy mining days, an establishment called the House of Lords on Main Street advertised "fine cuisine, gambling and 'soiled doves.'" Today the site of the notorious House of Lords is a city park, and most of what was downtown Joplin long ago moved to outlying malls. A few cafés, taverns, and specialty shops still serve the downtown area, but most of these struggle to survive.

STATE LINE MERCANTILE COMPANY, JOPLIN
c. 1946

The first business to occupy this property was a small gas station known as the Gray and Archer Filling Station. The business began as a one-room station with canopy in 1925. The original building housing the station was located at the right and was the width of the canopy. The much larger section of the building to the left was added at a later date.

In 1933, national prohibition was repealed, but liquor laws in Kansas continued to be fraught with complicated restrictions. It wasn't until November 1987 that an amendment to the Kansas state constitution allowed counties to choose "wet" or "dry" status. This hard-line stand on alcohol turned the Kansas–Missouri state line into a hotbed of activity. Twangs of country music poured from nightclubs and liquor flowed into every glass on the Missouri side of the line. For many Kansas residents, Route 66 was their link to a new world where you could enter a restaurant or bar and purchase liquor by the glass. Established in 1925, the State Line Bar and Grill just to the west of the mercantile was the first alcohol available to Kansans crossing the state line here. Directly across Route 66 from the mercantile was a very popular nightclub called the Oasis. Major country music acts of the day made the Oasis a regular stop on their tour schedules. The Shady Rest Motel, Gillead's Barbeque, and several other businesses also made the state-line area seem more like its own small town than a part of the west end of Joplin.

In 1979, the Paddoc family purchased the mercantile business, and it continues to operate as Paddoc State Line Liquor. Out front of Paddoc's are two old-style gravity pumps that hearken back to the days when gas flowed from the station and the area buzzed with activity. Inside are a liquor store and a bar patronized mostly by locals.

The state line area today is quiet and serene, a mere ghost of its storied past. The Oasis was destroyed by fire long ago, and the Shady Rest Motel and Gillead's Barbeque are but distant memories.

Of the 2,400 miles of Route 66 from Chicago to Los Angeles, Kansas accounts for a mere 13.2 miles. While cattle and the railroad played major roles in the economics of the region, this area of the state was ore-mining country from 1876 to around 1960. One lucky miner is said to have uncovered his fortune while sliding into first base during a baseball game. He quickly covered it up, leased the land that night, and began digging the next morning.

The first town one encounters along Route 66 in Kansas is Galena. Just before entering Galena is an area that looks a bit like a war-torn battle zone. Known as "Hell's Half Acre," piles of mining debris known as "chat" fill the landscape, a sobering reminder of past mining operations and the devastation it caused to the local environment. Many bloody union battles were also staged and fought in the region.

Just a few miles down 66 is Riverton, the onetime home of the world-famous Spring River Inn. Built in 1905, the Spring River began operation as a restaurant in 1952 and was destroyed by fire in the late 1990s. Still farther down the highway is Baxter Springs, "The First Cow Town in Kansas" and the site of the Baxter Springs Massacre. In October 1863 Lieutenant William Quantrill's Confederate troops, dressed in Union Army uniforms, ambushed an unknowing Union detachment and wagon train approaching the fort. One hundred three Union soldiers were killed, along with three Confederate soldiers. All are buried in a mass grave near the former site of the fort.

This part of Kansas boasts an abundance of rich and colorful history in which U.S Highway 66 played a major part. Tales of outlaw legends abound in these parts, including a well-known Jesse James bank robbery in the 1870s and frequent appearances by Bonnie Parker and Clyde Barrow more than 60 years later.

As the mining industry slowly dwindled the economy was bolstered by the influx of westbound travelers on Route 66. All three Kansas towns located along the Mother Road served travelers well. Those 13.2 miles in Kansas provide a virtual microcosm of the entire eight-state route; Galena, Riverton, and Baxter Springs were prime examples of the hundreds of small towns that dotted the length of the highway. During the Mother Road's heyday, their main streets were full of tourists filling their automobiles with gas or catching a quick bite at local cafés. Today, the streets are lined with classic architecture. Many a weary traveler too tired to drive another couple of miles to Oklahoma spent the night at Jayhawk Court in Riverton or the Capistrano Courts or Baxter Modern Cabins in Baxter Springs.

The lucrative tourist trade came to a sudden end when Interstate construction was completed in the area in the early 1960s, connecting I-44 in Missouri to the Will Rogers Turnpike in Oklahoma and leaving Kansas high and dry. In fact, Kansas holds the dubious distinction of being the only Route 66 state to be completely bypassed by the Interstate. It is also the only state not represented in Bobby Troup's hit song "Get Your Kicks on Route 66." The old route through Kansas remained a state road, however, and is today designated Kansas 66. Local residents are proud of their 13.2 miles and work hard to keep and preserve what is left.

GALENA

c. 1950s

Route 66 enters Galena over a gracefully curved overpass down to Front Street. After about half a mile, it takes a sharp left-hand turn onto Main Street. At one time Galena, named for a type of lead ore that often contained silver, had a reputation as a rowdy, untamed mining town complete with gamblers, swindlers, and drunkards. Main Street during the early 1900s mining boom was known as "Red Hot Street" and was full of saloons, gambling joints, and bawdy houses, all open 24 hours. Traveling down the sleepy Main Street today one would be hard-pressed to see any evidence of Galena's wild past. In 1935 striking United Mine Workers blocked Route 66 in front of the Eagle Picher Smelter and shot at drivers who ignored their commands. Sheriffs rerouted traffic and the governor declared martial law and sent in the National Guard. Labor unrest continued and reached a climax in 1937 when nine men were shot while demonstrating against union organization efforts. During the 1940s and 1950s local roadside businesses enjoyed steady streams of traffic and customers as America's Main Street also happened to be Galena's Main Street. Today, Main Street is home to a few local businesses but the damage caused by a dwindling mining industry and a Route 66 bypass is evident in the abandoned brick buildings that line the street. During the mining boom Galena's population ran as high as 25,000; today it hovers at around 4,000.

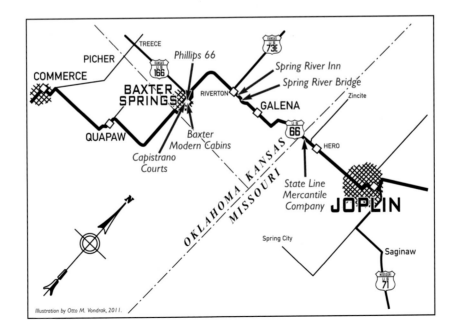

Illustration by Otto M. Vondrak, 2011.

SPRING RIVER BRIDGE, RIVERTON
c. 1926

Built in 1922 by the Marsh Bridge Company, the Spring River Bridge was an elegant three-span structure designed by James B. Marsh, who began a professional career as a bridge designer with the King Bridge Company of Cleveland, Ohio, in 1883. During his tenure with the King Bridge Company, which was one of the largest in the United States at that time, Marsh also became the head of the Northern Agency for the Kansas City Bridge and Iron Company, where he not only was a key designer, but also oversaw construction.

By March 1889 Marsh had become general western agent and contracting engineer for the King Bridge Company and was placed in charge of the general western office in Des Moines, Iowa. In the spring of 1896 he formed his own company, the Marsh Bridge Company, and at the turn of the century began to design bridges utilizing a steel skeleton structure encased in concrete, which gave his bridges their unique and graceful look.

In April 1904 the Marsh Bridge Company was incorporated as the Marsh Engineering Company, and in 1912 Marsh was awarded a patent for the Marsh Rainbow Arch Bridge, a design that became a favorite with state engineers and county commissioners. The bridge could be built using inexpensive materials, and it was durable, aesthetically pleasing, and virtually maintenance free. A standard Marsh bridge consisted of one to three arches, although they have been built using as many as 11 arches. The earliest known Marsh bridge in Kansas was built in 1917, and the last was erected in 1934. Construction of the arch bridges reached its peak in the late 1920s and declined after 1930.

In 1986, too narrow to handle the modern traffic flow and simply obsolete, the Spring River Bridge was dismantled. The Willow Creek Bridge near Baxter Springs met its end on November 11, 1991. The only remaining Marsh bridge on Route 66 rests a couple of miles west of Riverton over Brush Creek. Built in 1923, the single-span Brush Creek Bridge was listed on the National Register of Historic Places in 1983. It was slated for demolition in the mid-1990s, but the combined preservation efforts of the Kansas Route 66 Association, the Cherokee County Commission, and protesters from around the world saved it. The Brush Creek Bridge was fully restored. Today it stands as a testament to its designer and as a memorial to the millions of motorists who traveled her during the glory days of the Mother Road.

SPRING RIVER INN, RIVERTON
c. 1960

Traveling eastward across the Spring River Bridge, one encountered the entrance to the historic Spring River Inn. In the early years of Missouri's statehood, this area along the banks of the Spring River was declared a no man's land and a no-fighting zone for Missouri citizens and the Cherokee nation. By 1869 this buffer zone was no longer necessary and the land was opened to settlers.

In 1902 B. F. Steward built a private residence on a parcel of land along the edge of the Spring River and thus laid the groundwork for the Spring River Inn. On July 24, 1905, Steward sold his home to the Country Club of Joplin, Missouri. The club became the social center of the area and was so popular that it was a regular stop on the Joplin trolley line. In 1913 the Country Club boasted an early version of a built-in swimming pool known as a swimming tank. Only 4 feet deep, the pool's abandoned foundation still sits a few hundred yards northeast of the inn.

The Spring River Inn was situated on 7 ½ acres and included tennis courts, picnic areas, and boating facilities. When the Depression hit in the 1930s, the club fell on hard times. In 1932 club president J. W. Grantham bought the building and used it for several years as a summer home with his wife, Cora Pearl. The Granthams regularly entertained theater celebrities there as actors made their way through Joplin and Baxter Springs on tour. After only a few years, however, the home stood vacant, abandoned, and all but forgotten.

Thankfully the inn was purchased and saved by June and Gates Harrold in 1952. They fully converted to a large restaurant with six private dining areas, including a room to seat over 350 guests. From 1970 until 1994 Judy and Ray Birk owned and operated the Spring River Inn. On November 1, 1994, partners David and Kay Graham and Dewayne and Lavern Treece purchased the inn. The Spring River Inn was well known for its 35-foot all-you-can-eat buffet, a culinary delight loaded with delicious home-cooked food and desserts, including two trademark specialties: cinnamon pull-apart bread and squaw bread.

The Spring River Inn closed in 1996 and met its permanent demise in a fire that completely destroyed the building on October 20, 1998.

EISLER BROTHERS MARKET, RIVERTON
c. 1930s

On March 20, 1925 Leo Williams and his wife Lora opened a small roadside store on what was to become U.S. Highway 66 through Riverton. Fashioned after the "general" stores of the era, the Williams' store carried everything from clothes and shoes to milk, eggs, and fresh meat, as well as chili and barbecued beef that were cooked in a pit out back. A regulation croquet court was built on a lot adjacent to the store complete with lights for night play. Local tournaments became popular among area residents. As traffic continued to grow, business flourished and the court was dismantled to accommodate a parking lot.

In 1945 Leo leased the store to Lloyd Paxton and purchased a roller rink in nearby Galena. When Paxton's lease expired, Lora, then a widow, returned to manage the store as Lora Williams' AG Food Market. In 1971 Lora transferred ownership of the property to her daughter, Jane. Joe and Isabelle Eisler bought the business from Thelma Ball in 1973 and continue to operate it as a store and deli with nephew Scott Nelson (president of the Kansas Route 66 Association) as manager. Although Interstate 44 bypassed this area in 1961 the store continues to survive as a result of its strong local customer base and the current crop of Route 66 explorers.

U.S. 66 AND MAIN STREET   BAXTER SPRINGS, KANSAS   D-1

CAPISTRANO COURTS, BAXTER SPRINGS
c. 1948

The Capistrano Courts were built on the south edge of Baxter Springs sometime between 1948 and 1950. The motel covered an area the size of half a city block and was configured in an L shape. Capistrano Courts was built using stucco and resembled the Spanish adobe style common to many motels located farther west. The gabled roof over each entry was a deviation from the traditional adobe structure, however.

The Capistrano Courts comprised six buildings, each containing two units. Fully covered carports were situated between buildings; one guest unit from each building shared a common carport with the unit across from it. A sign depicting a swallow was erected roadside so one can assume that the Capistrano Courts were named for San Juan Capistrano, California, where cliff swallows return to nest every March. This theme was very fitting for a motel where repeat business year after year was vitally important. Later, the word "Motel" was added beneath the colorful swallow. The change from "Courts" to "Motel"

was common practice by the late 1940s and gave the image of being more modern and up to date.

The Capistrano Motel was purchased by Orville and Phyliss Mehaffey in 1954. Orville and Phyliss made sure that the Capistrano had an outstanding reputation for cleanliness, knowing that a clean haven would go a long way in attracting tourists. They also treated their guests to a continental breakfast, a common perk utilized by the larger motel chains but less common with the smaller "mom-and-pop" motels. A children's playground was also added during the time the Mehaffeys owned the motel.

Orville and Phyliss managed the motel until 1977, when it was sold to Mr. and Mrs. Harry Miller, who operated and cared for the motel until 1987. Sadly, the Capistrano Motel was razed in 1988. A liquor store now sits on a small portion of the half-block area that the Capistrano Motel once filled.

BAXTER MODERN CABINS, BAXTER SPRINGS
c. 1947

Built in the mid-1940s, this classic U-shaped motel consisted of 12 guest rooms and a gas station that doubled as the motel office. Each gable-roofed unit was connected to a covered carport that featured an unusual semicircle façade. Legend has it that two married lovers who were carrying on an illicit affair made the motel their usual meeting place. One evening a faulty natural gas line filled their room with gas, and they never awoke from their blissful sleep. They were found the next morning together in bed, much to the dismay of their respective spouses.

Highway 66 through Kansas comprised just slightly more than 13 miles of roadway, but provided a microcosm of the entire route. Service stations, cafés, and motels, as well as various stands and shops, were located all along those 13 miles. Most are long gone, as are the Baxter Modern Cabins, which closed around 1965. A faceless Wal-Mart now sits on the former site of the motel where travelers and the occasional star-crossed couple sought refuge. If you tend to believe in such things as ghosts, you have to wonder if the two lost souls, hopelessly in love, are endlessly wandering the store aisles searching for a way out.

Route 66 was born in Oklahoma and its father was Cyrus Avery, a Tulsa businessman who became the state's first highway commissioner in 1913. After several years of lobbying for a national highway system, his hard work and perseverance paid off. In 1925 a letter from U.S. Secretary of Agriculture Howard Gore announcing the creation of a special board to "design and number a system of routes of interstate and national importance" arrived at his door. Gore asked Avery to act as a consultant to the American Association of State Highway Officials, which Avery persuaded to route the new highway through Oklahoma, Texas, New Mexico, Arizona, and into California. Prior to Avery's lobbying the new highway's path was to travel through Kansas and Colorado on its way to California. After much debate, Avery also convinced the board to settle on the number 66 for the new Chicago-to-Los Angeles highway.

In the early 1930s drought, dust storms, and the Great Depression triggered a mass migration of Texas, Arkansas, Kansas, and Colorado farmers to head for California's promised land. More than 200,000 of these Dust Bowl migrants fled through Oklahoma on Highway 66. John Steinbeck, in his Pulitzer Prize–winning novel, *The Grapes of Wrath,* forever immortalized to the world the plight of the Oklahoma farmer or "Okie." One can hardly forget the visual impact characterized in John Ford's motion picture adaptation of three generations of the Joad family, tightly packed into their cut-down Hudson Super Six sedan, and struggling to cross the dry plains, desert, and mountains to reach California. "66 is the path of a people in flight, refugees from dust and shrinking land, from the thunder of tractors and shrinking ownership," wrote Steinbeck, "they come into 66 from the tributary side roads, from the wagon tracks and the rutted country roads. 66 is the mother road, the road of flight."

The Turner Turnpike (Interstate 44) between Tulsa and Oklahoma City, bypassed 100 miles of the Mother Road and was the first major bypass on the route. In 1957 the Will Rogers Turnpike opened between Tulsa and Miami, leaving another 100 miles of Route 66 to fend for itself. In 1975 the four-lane section of Route 66 from Sayre to Erick was the last section in Oklahoma to lose its U.S. 66 designation to I-40.

The pathway of Route 66 in Oklahoma covers approximately 400 miles and travels somewhat diagonally across the heart of the state, slicing through mining, agricultural, industrial, and oil regions. Although 66 went through countless changes over the years in Oklahoma, there are still more drivable "original" portions of Route 66 in that state than any other.

MIAMI
c. 1930s

Miami, Oklahoma, was established in 1891. That much is certain. How it got its name is a different matter. Some say Wayland C. Lykins, a cattle rancher attracted to the region's plentiful grazing land got the townsite approved, and on March 2, 1891, Miami became the first chartered town in "Indian Territory," named by Lykins for the local tribe. Others say Miami started out as a trading post called "Jimtown" because it was near the homes of four local farmers named Jim. In 1890 to expedite mail delivery, arrangements were made with one of the farmers, Jim Palmer, to establish a post office. The name Miami was chosen in honor of Palmer's wife, who was of Miami Indian blood. No matter which story you believe, remember: Miami is pronounced *my-am-uh* not *my-am-ee*.

In 1922, a unique stretch of roadway was built between Miami and Afton. When it came time to pave the 10 miles between the two cities, the highway commissioners from Craig and Ottawa counties found they had half the money necessary. Since the Federal Highway Commission required the road to be paved for the county to receive federal funds but did not specify width, engineer George Klein suggested they make the road a single lane 9 feet wide paved all the way. In 1937, this stretch was finally bypassed and became the last section of Route 66 in Oklahoma to be completely paved. Portions of this so-called "Ribbon Highway" or "Sidewalk Highway" can still be driven today.

THE COLEMAN THEATER, MIAMI
c. 1939

The beautifully opulent Coleman Theater sits on Main Street in Miami, Oklahoma, on what was once Route 66. It was built in 1929 at a cost of $590,000 by George L. Coleman Sr., who made his fortune mining zinc and lead in the area. Coleman handed over the designing chores to the Boller Brothers of Kansas City, Missouri, who came up with the majestic Spanish-Colonial design, complete with hand-carved gargoyles and figurines. The interior is of Louis XV design and features gold-leaf trim, stained-glass windows, and carved mahogany railings and moldings.

Vaudeville was the entertainment of the time, and the Coleman opened to a sellout crowd on April 18, 1929. Patrons paid $1 each for admission. Since then, the Coleman has hosted many well-known performers, including Will Rogers and the infamous fan dancer Sally Rand. By the dawn of the 1940s, vaudeville had fallen out of favor, and the Coleman began showing the latest in motion pictures. In 1983 it was listed on the National Register of Historic Places, and it was donated to the city of Miami by the Coleman family in 1989. By 1990 movies were no longer shown at the Coleman except for the occasional revival classic. Friends of the Coleman was founded in 1992 to preserve the legacy of the theater and restore the Coleman to its original grandeur.

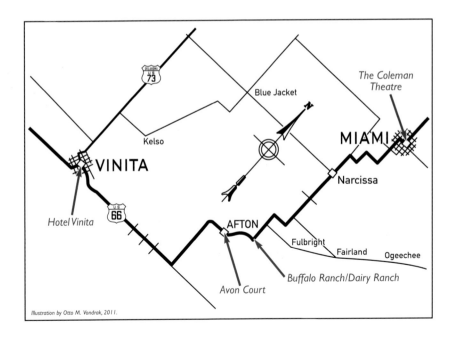

Illustration by Otto M. Vondrak, 2011.

BUFFALO RANCH/DAIRY RANCH, AFTON
c. 1959

Russell and Aleene Kay opened the Buffalo Ranch on July 11, 1953, after two years of searching for the perfect location to establish a tourist business. They eventually decided on this portion of land in northeast Oklahoma near Afton where Highways 69, 60, and 66 merged. From the beginning the couple decided to raise buffalo as part of their trading-post business. They opened the Ranch with a budget of $5,000 and seven head of bison. The business prospered over the next few years and grew with the addition of a Western store (billed as the world's largest), a barbecue restaurant, and an ice cream parlor. The Chuck Wagon barbecue restaurant accommodated 65 to 70 people; customers sat on benches at long tables and helped themselves to a family-style buffet. The Dairy Ranch ice cream parlor, which opened around 1954, served simpler fare, including burgers, fries, and ice cream treats. In 1958 the Dairy Ranch was purchased by Betty Wheatley, who ran the store until the end of the 2000 summer season.

Over the years the Buffalo Ranch became a very popular tourist stop, as thousands of travelers heading west jumped at the chance to stop and see the wild bison and purchase souvenirs. The Buffalo Ranch was most successful during the peak operating season, which lasted from Memorial Day to Labor Day. During that time the Buffalo Ranch sponsored Indian tribal dances to attract tourists. Most of the dancers lived in small huts on the property. Rabbits and chickens, as well as larger livestock such as llamas, elk, deer, sheep, and goats, were added to the menagerie, and the bison herd topped out at 40 head. There was never a charge to view the animals.

In 1963 Russell Kay passed away and left Aleene alone to operate the Buffalo Ranch. She admitted that it was a terrible struggle at first, but she persevered. The Will Rogers Turnpike (Interstate 44) bypassed Route 66 in this area in 1957, but the Buffalo Ranch complex held its ground and continued operating until Aleene's death in 1997. Sadly, the stock and furnishings were auctioned off on April 4, 1998, and the Buffalo Ranch was eventually bulldozed. A modern travel center now sits on the property. The new owner still calls the business the Buffalo Ranch and has even acquired a few buffalo in an effort to keep the legacy alive.

AFTON
c. 1958

The small farming community of Afton was established in 1886 and given its name by railroad surveyor Anton Aires, who named the town after his daughter. Afton has many historic buildings lining its downtown area, including the old Palmer Hotel and the Rest Haven Motel. The Interstate bypass in 1957 and the decommissioning of Route 66 had a profoundly negative impact on Afton's economy. During the golden era of U.S. Highway 66, Afton was a thriving community with no less than six service stations and six motels lining its short stretch of Main Street. Today, there are very few survivors. On the outskirts of town stands the venerable Buffalo Ranch Trading Post, a landmark tourist stop built in 1953 by Russell and Aleene Kay with a budget of $5,000. The business eventually grew to include four buildings housing a trading post, western store, barbecue, dairy ranch, and a variety of livestock. The Buffalo Ranch closed its doors in 1997 when owner Aleene Albro (then remarried) died. The original buildings were torn down in 2002 and replaced with a new facility that includes a gas station and restaurant.

Afton is also home to Afton Station. From 1999 to the time of this writing, Laurel Kane has been restoring the 1930s-era gas station for use as a Route 66 visitors' center. Every attempt is being made to preserve the vintage flavor of the old service station, which originally sold Sunray DX petroleum products. An attached garage will serve as a museum for vintage automobiles.

Avon Court
Hi-ways 69-66-60-59, Afton, Okla.
W. R. Trebilcock, Prop.

AVON COURT, AFTON
c. 1951

John Foley built the Avon Court in 1936 on the west end of the small town of Afton. It was a relatively small motel, consisting of just seven units. Each unit was built with its own covered carport, a common guest convenience for motels of that era. "Panel Ray Heat, Air Cooled, Clean, Comfortable Reasonable Rates and a Modern Trailer Park" were all part of the advertised amenities.

The Avon Court changed hands several times. At the time this postcard was made, it was owned and operated by W. R. Trebilcock, who bought the property in 1951 and operated it until 1955, when he sold it to Harry Glover. The interstate bypass was built in 1957, and in 1958 Glover sold the property. Although barren and empty, the skeletons of three units still stand today, providing a brief glimpse into a long-gone era.

During the heyday of Route 66, Afton was a beehive of activity, boasting several service stations, cafés, and motels. The bypass had a devastating impact on the town and its economy, making Afton an archetypal example of the damage done by the super slab.

VINITA
c. 1939

Vinita, Oklahoma is not only the oldest incorporated town in Oklahoma, it is the second oldest town in the state. Vinita was established in 1871 and, like so many other towns in this part of Oklahoma, was primarily known as a railroad community. Originally known as Downingville, the name was later changed to honor Vinnie Ream, the local sculptress commissioned to carve the statue of Abraham Lincoln now located in the U.S. Capitol Building in Washington, D.C. Colonel Elias C. Boudinot, a Cherokee and one of the town site's first promoters, was responsible for the name change. Boudinot's father and 34 others were responsible for selling the Cherokee ancestral lands in the Southeast to the federal government.

The Trail of Tears mass migration that resulted in 1838 brought thousands of relocated Cherokees to the area.

Several historic buildings survive in Vinita, including the fully restored shopping district. Vinita is also home to Clanton's Café, built in 1927 and now being run by the fourth generation of Clantons. Hotel Vinita and the Spraker Service Station also served Route 66 during its heyday and were added to the National Register of Historic Places in 1995. In addition, Will Rogers went to the Willie Halsell Institute in Vinita, and it's said that he felt more at home there than at any other school he attended.

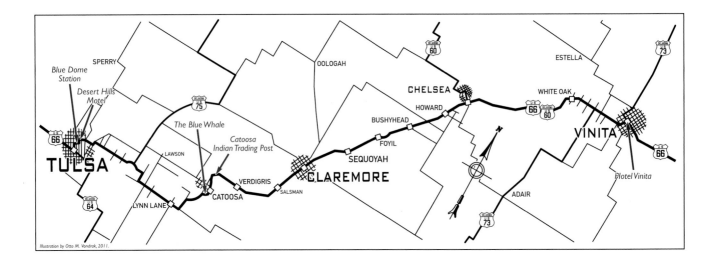

Illustration by Otto M. Vondrak, 2011.

DESERT HILLS MOTEL, TULSA
c. 1953

In 1933 the path of Highway 66 entering Tulsa from the east was routed down Eleventh Street, much to the delight of local businesses. Cafés, motels, and service stations sprang up along the entire stretch of Eleventh Street into downtown Tulsa. In 1953 the Desert Hills Motel and its often-photographed classic neon sign were erected just 10 minutes from downtown. The motel is set up in a U shape that consists of 50 units and an office. The motel boasted individually air-conditioned units, wall-to-wall carpeting, and free radio and television. Guests were also treated to free morning coffee served in the lobby. At one time the amenities included a pool, but it has long since been filled in.

By 1973 the Tulsa area and the Desert Hills Motel were completely bypassed, and the motel struggled to survive. What followed the bypass is a story similar to those of hundreds of motels along Route 66. As tourist traffic faded, rooms became weekly and monthly rental units, and dollars once spent on upkeep and maintenance became nonexistent.

In 1996 Jack Patel bought the Desert Hills Motel with a desire to restore it to its former glory. "When I bought the motel, only 25 rooms were in operating condition," he says. He meticulously renovated each room until all 50 were guest ready. For now the classic neon sign continues to light up Tulsa's evening sky, its warm inviting glow enticing rest-starved travelers to enjoy a quiet night's sleep within.

BLUE DOME STATION, TULSA
c. 1949

T. J. Chastain built the Blue Dome station in 1925 on the corner of Second Street and Elgin Avenue. Chastain was the owner and manager of the Chastain Oil Company, a large manufacturer and distributor of petroleum products in the Tulsa region, and the Blue Dome was his first effort to expand his business interests by adding retail outlets for his own Superoil products. A business associate suggested that the domes around the station be painted blue and the station be called the Blue Dome. Chastain did not take to the idea at first, but eventually changed his mind, and the name stuck.

The station originally sold and distributed Chastain's own Superoil products. But in 1928 Chastain procured the Tulsa County rights to Tydol Oil and sold Tydol Gasoline and Veedol Motor Oil alongside Superoil. Later on, Gulf Oil products were sold at the station.

The Blue Dome is said to be the first station in Oklahoma to provide such customer conveniences as hot water, pressurized air, and the until-then-unheard-of car wash. It was a huge success and one of the highest-grossing stations in the entire region, open 24 hours a day, 7 days a week. Upstairs in the dome itself, accessed by a spiral staircase, there was a small living space for the manager. In 1928 a second station was built at Fourth Street and Detroit Avenue. The original Blue Dome is being restored and is one of many Art Deco treasures found in the Tulsa area.

THE BLUE DOME, "BEST IN WEST", 2nd AND ELGIN, TULSA, OKLA. ~ 1949, ROUTE 66

SHADY REST COURT, WEST TULSA
c. 1942

The Shady Rest Court is located in West Tulsa in what was once a suburb called Red Fork. Maurice Colpitts, a Tulsa plumbing inspector, built the front-gable-style Shady Rest Cabins in 1936. Each of the 13 units was built around a 10x12-foot frame just large enough for a bed and two people. Unlike those at many motels, the Shady Rest carports were never converted to rooms, adding to the historic value and vintage feel. During the glory days of Route 66 the Shady Rest Court offered "The best of accommodations for your money. Innerspring mattresses and air cooled cabins."

Unfortunately, restoration plans that got under way in 2003 didn't last long. In a story all too familiar among classic Route 66 motels, this onetime safe haven for travelers had turned into a seedy flophouse, and in 2005 local authorities pulled the plug on the venerable old motor court. A few weeks later the Shady Rest Court was bulldozed.

In a way, it's nice to see old classics that have fallen into such disrepair taken out of their miserable states and put to rest. Colpitts, I am sure, would heartily agree.

SHADY REST COURT
TULSA, OKLAHOMA

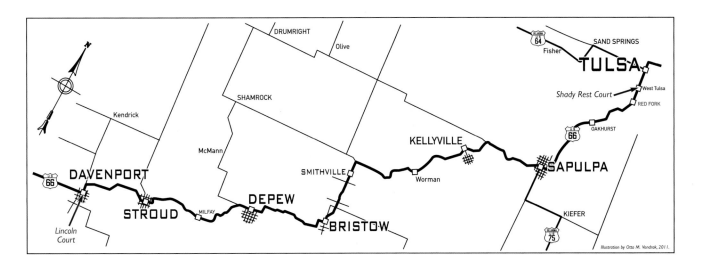

Illustration by Otto M. Vondrak, 2011.

RED FORK, OKLAHOMA
c. 1949

Red Fork was founded sometime during the 1880s south of the Arkansas River just southwest of Tulsa. Named for the Red Fork of the Arkansas River, it was typical of frontier towns in its day. The entire territory was established to relocate Native American tribes who moved into the region after the passage of the Indian Removal Act of 1830. In 1901, oil was discovered in Red Fork and would forever change the surrounding area. Although the Red Fork oilfield discovery fell far short of its anticipated output, it nevertheless put the surrounding area on the oil map. A few years later in 1905, on a farm 12 miles south of the city, a much larger field known as Glenn Pool was discovered, and Tulsa was soon proclaimed the Oil Capital of the World.

During World War II, Red Fork became home to many of the region's manufacturing plants. Jack D. Rittenhouse, in his 1946 book,

A Guide Book to Highway 66, describes Red Fork as an "industrial suburb of Tulsa containing many factories." The world famous Frankhoma pottery plant is located in Red Fork.

Southwest Boulevard, the road that would eventually carry Highway 66 through Red Fork, was fully paved in 1922, four years prior to the official designation of the new highway. In 1959, Route 66 through the area was moved onto Interstate 44. Old 66 leaving Tulsa on Southwest Boulevard via Red Fork became Business 66, a designation that ended at the I-44/I-244 junction prior to entering Oakhurst. As time went on, the boundaries separating the communities of Red Fork and Tulsa vanished and Red Fork was eventually consumed by Tulsa's growth, becoming part of the expanding metropolitan area.

LINCOLN COURT, CHANDLER
c. 1939

Joe Gibson began his venture into the auto court business in the early 1930s when he built Gibson's Modern Camp and Apartments. This early roadside business was located in Chandler near the railroad station and included a gas station, auto court, and café. A member of the United Auto Courts, Gibson's offered accommodations ranging from $1 to $3 per night depending on room size and amenities.

In 1939, Gibson built the 16-room Lincoln Court on a piece of land on the east end of Chandler, hoping to cash in on the increase in tourist travel. Gibson placed eight bungalows on his property, each housing two guest rooms. In 1969, a brick building was erected at the front of the property, adding an additional four units and increasing the room total to 20. Truck parking was located in the rear of the property, and a restaurant was conveniently located next door to keep the hungry travelers happy.

The main floor area of each room's interior was finished with polished wood while the bathroom was finished with vinyl flooring. All of the original wood flooring and vinyl still exists and is meticulously maintained by current owner, Mike Patel, who purchased the motel in 1980 and is adamant about keeping the Lincoln and its surroundings spotless and in pristine period condition. The exterior of the motel's buildings was originally white and had "already been painted brown by the time I bought the motel," Mike told me. Exterior color scheme aside, walking the motel and its grounds is like stepping back in time. In case you get nervous and think you've entered some sort of time warp, just take a deep breath and shoot a glance toward 66. The modern autos should snap you back.

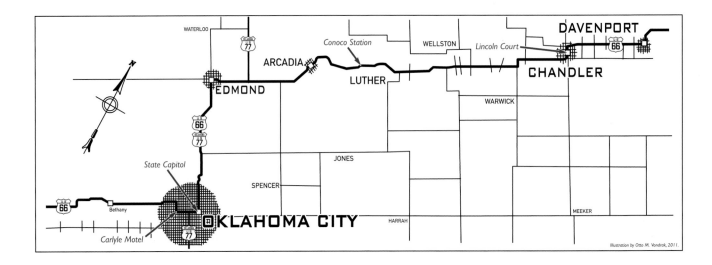

Illustration by Otto M. Vondrak, 2011.

CHANDLER
c. 1940

Named for U.S. Assistant Secretary of the Interior George Chandler, the town of Chandler was established in September 1891, when its first post office opened its doors. Six years later, a ferocious tornado ripped through the town, destroying most of the structures and killing 14 people. The town's citizens banded together and quickly began rebuilding Chandler. Twelve of the rebuilt structures are listed on the National Register of Historic Places, including the Wolcott Building (City Drug Store) and the St. Cloud Hotel, both on Manvel Avenue.

Chandler is also home to a 1930s-style Phillips 66 service station. Located at Seventh and Manvel, the station has been undergoing restoration for the past several years. Bill Fernau, the owner of the property, hopes not only to fully restore it but also to turn it into a working station.

William Tilgham served as sheriff of Chandler from 1901 to 1905 and was a deputy to Bat Masterson. Tilgham became a state senator in 1910 and returned to active duty as a sheriff in nearby Cromwell in 1924. On November 1 of that same year, he was killed in what is considered the last gunfight of the Old West. He was laid to rest in a local Chandler cemetery.

When Route 66 was designated to run through Chandler in 1926, Manvel Avenue, the town's main street, was paved with brick and was actually one of the few "hard" roads in the area. Oklahoma was then known for its vast, rich oil fields, and Chandler was regarded as the gateway into the state's oil country. Oil pumps, or "grasshoppers," are still a very common sight on Route 66 from Chandler west to Oklahoma City and beyond. This region is also known as pecan country. At one time so many pecans were grown here that Chandler was known as the "Pecan Capital of the World."

The Turner Turnpike (I-44) bypassed Chandler in 1953, but the townspeople took it in stride. Despite the setback, the community continued to grow and develop.

CONOCO STATION, ARCADIA
c. 1940

It is believed that this primitive stone station was built between 1915 and the very early 1920s. Its location was so remote that electricity was never run to the building. Kerosene lamps were used for lighting instead, compounding the dangers already involved in dispensing gasoline. The station also sold oil and kerosene, which were dispensed from large metal drums with only simple spigots to control the flow.

Local legend has it that the owners were involved in counterfeiting U.S. currency. Times were tough during the 1930s, so when a "salesman" paid a visit and offered a way to make a lot of quick cash, the temptation was too much. The story goes that the owners purchased a set of printing plates to make bogus $10 bills and even added a tiny room to the back of the station to serve as a print shop. The room was well disguised; its only entrance was a window on the back wall. Eventually the counterfeit bills were traced back to the station, where the plates were found, and the owners were arrested and sent to prison. The station was closed, never to open again. The stone ruins remain, seemingly daring time and the elements to take their best shot. My 10 bucks are on the stone.

VIEW FROM THE
CAPITOL BUILDING, OKLAHOMA CITY
c. 1935

Route 66 carried motorists directly in front of the Capitol Building in Oklahoma City, the only state capital on the entire route, via Lincoln Boulevard. Oklahoma City became the largest boomtown of the 1889 Land Rush when the region was opened for white settlement despite the promise of being "forever" set aside as "Indian Territory." On April 22 of that year, more than 10,000 people flocked to an area known as the Cherokee Strip between noon and sundown to stake claim to their land. Many of the settlers illegally camped out beforehand, hoping to get an advantage on the competition. These early birds were given the name "Sooners," a nickname still applied to University of Oklahoma sports teams and the state nickname "The Sooner State." A second boom took place during the depression years when oil was struck in the area. By 1946, more than 1,000 oil derricks were located in and around the city, many of which still produce oil to this day. Most of the vintage Route 66 charm in Oklahoma City is long gone, the cafés, diners, classic service stations, and motor courts but a fond memory. But if you spend time and look hard enough, there are still remnants of the Mother Road waiting to be discovered in Oklahoma City.

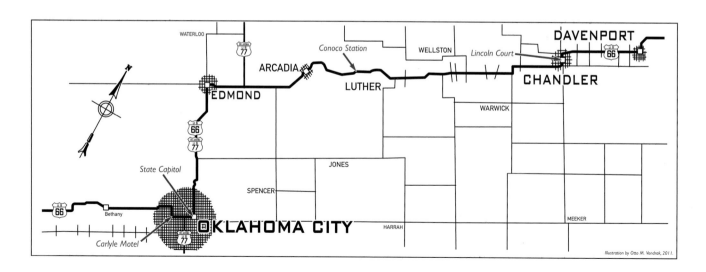

Illustration by Otto M. Vondrak, 2011.

CARLYLE MOTEL, OKLAHOMA CITY
c. 1965

Lyle and Ruby Overman arrived in Oklahoma City from St. Louis, Missouri, in 1940 after selling the Trav-O-Tel Motel, which they built in 1938. Not discouraged by the setbacks they faced with the Trav-O-Tel due to the often-flooded Meramec River, the Overmans built two new motels on the western edge of Oklahoma City. The first was the Major Court; the second, built in 1943, was dubbed Carlyle Court.

Not having much space on which to build the Carlyle, the Overmans decided to forgo the private garages that were part of the Major Court and a popular amenity of many motels at that time.

This decision gave them more space and allowed the Overmans to squeeze more guest units onto the site. The final plan was to build six small, ranch-style buildings with three guest units in each building. Three of the ranch-style buildings sit on each side of the property, angled toward the front in an overlapping configuration. The office and manager's residence sits centered at the front of the property.

By 1956, the AAA-rated Carlyle Motel offered air conditioning, wall-to-wall carpets, and a playground for the kids. A swimming pool was added later in the courtyard space between the two sets of

units. Cribs were also an amenity provided to guests, just in time for the baby boom.

In 1994, Tom Patel purchased the Carlyle Motel and has been greeting overnight guests ever since. Tom told me that 250 to 300 people traveling Route 66 stay at the Carlyle every year. He would like to see more but believes gas prices might be keeping people away. He also says that the neon sign out front is a big attraction for Route 66 tourists. The neon is still lit at night, but the city made him remove the sign's attention-getting flashing feature, citing it as a distraction for drivers. Wasn't getting your attention the idea in the first place?

YUKON
c. 1949

Railroad builder A. N. Spencer owned the 160-acre site on which the town of Yukon was built and established in 1891. Spencer was busy building a railroad, so he brought in his brothers, L. M. Spencer, Sam Spencer, and William Spencer, to help build the town. The brothers named the town for the Yukon River in Alaska.

For many years, wheat and the railroad were the bread and butter of Yukon's economy. Those days have slowly drifted into distant memory, but Yukon's Best Flour grain elevators still survive and are a Route 66 landmark at the east end of town on Main Street. Directly across from the grain elevators on the north side of Main is Yukon's Best Railroad Museum, housed in fully restored boxcars. The museum also boasts of a substantial Route 66 exhibit.

The town grew slowly and was finally incorporated in 1901. In 1910, the city voted to build a sewer system and supply running water to its residents. Highway 66 came through in 1926, and by 1928, the two-lane highway through town was paved with Portland concrete or asphalt. Highway 66 had the honor of becoming the first road to see pavement in Yukon, and by 1958, Route 66 through town was a fully paved, modern four-lane highway.

In the days prior to Yukon's incorporation, the historic Chisholm Trail sliced through this area and provided the pathway for ranchers driving cattle east from Texas during the 1870s and 1880s. The Chisholm Trail crosses paths with Route 66 at 9th Street in Yukon and continues its path down 9th Street as it makes its way out of the city. At the city park, an 1870s-era watering hole, a historic marker commemorates the landmark trail. As you enter the city you will notice signs boasting Yukon to be the home of country megastar Garth Brooks. Although he was born in Tulsa, Garth was raised in Yukon.

HINTON JUNCTION COURTS & CAFÉ, HINTON JUNCTION
c. 1951

The Hinton Junction Café was built by E. B. Enze and was located just west of the pony-truss bridge that currently carries traffic over the South Canadian River. Officially known as the William H. Murray Bridge, the pony truss replaced the Key Toll Bridge when Highway 66 was rerouted away from Calumet, Geary, and Bridgeport in 1934.

Leon Little, who owned a succession of tourist facilities in the area, including a gas station near the Key Toll Bridge, moved this business when Highway 66 was rerouted. In 1943, after being drafted, Little leased his business to Enze. In a shrewd business move, Enze shut down Little's facility and opened a café and gas station of his own nearby. The lease was up soon after the war, and

Little and his wife, Ann, returned to pick up where they had left off, reopening their gas station and café.

Enze's business thrived during the late 1940s and 1950s, pumping gasoline 24 hours a day and serving food. A small motel with four rooms was added in a building at the back of the property. This motel portion of the business eventually expanded to include "ten modern cabins with individual air conditioning and television," as the back of the period postcard states. Business was great until traffic moved from Highway 66 onto the interstate in 1962. The number of cars traveling Route 66 dwindled to almost nothing, forcing the eventual closure of both Enze's Hinton Junction Courts and Café and Little's Gas Station and Café.

KEY TOLL BRIDGE, GEARY
c. 1926

Built in 1921 over the South Canadian River, the Key Toll Bridge was named for its builder, local politician George D. Keys. Several predecessors to the Key Toll Bridge dated back to the late 1800s, but all met with disastrous ends, washed out by heavy rains and subsequent rushing high water. A high-water bridge was needed, and Keys was the man to get it done. The new suspension-style bridge swept 1,000 feet across the South Canadian River, connecting the towns of Geary and Bridgeport.

In November 1926 a jagged dirt road pathway from Calumet to Geary, as well as the bridge between Geary and Bridgeport, became parts of the new U.S Highway 66. Local support for the new highway was huge. Geary citizens were so enthused about the possibility of Highway 66 running through their town that hundreds volunteered to gravel and grade the road and thus ensure Geary's inclusion in the new highway. A free campground for travelers, sponsored and maintained by the Geary Businessmen's Club, was also built to attract business.

Despite public protest, the Key Bridge remained a toll crossing from its completion in 1921 until 1930. A tollbooth on the Geary side was manned and operated by William Phillips. He and his family lived on-site, and his wife sold sandwiches and snacks to passing motorists. Tolls ranged from 25 cents for horses to $1 for automobiles. A dollar was a steep price to pay in those days, but unless you were willing to travel 50 miles to the nearest reliable free crossing, you had no choice. Many a motorist was stranded when unable to pay the toll.

Continued protests rang loud. As a result, the bridge was purchased by the state of Oklahoma in 1930, and the toll was eliminated. Unfortunately for the citizens of Calumet, Geary, and Bridgeport, the utopia created by Highway 66 came to an early end. In October 1932 construction began on a new bridge 3 miles to the east of the Key Bridge. The new crossing would be part of a Highway 66 realignment that would bypass the three communities and connect El Reno and Hydro via a straight shot. On July 17, 1934, the El Reno Cut-Off was completed, and a reported 15,000 people attended a celebration at the new bridge.

The Key Bridge remained intact but was utilized for local traffic only. In 1946 fire severely damaged the Key Bridge and, due to costs, repair was out of the question. In 1952 the Key Bridge was sold to a Kansas City salvage company and was dismantled without fanfare shortly thereafter.

BRIDGEPORT BRIDGE

HAMONS' COURT
(AKA LUCILLE'S), HYDRO
c. 1941

The original two-story building that eventually housed Hamons' Gas Station was built in 1927 by a man named Carl Ditmore of Hydro, Oklahoma. After a couple of years a five-unit motel was built behind the station. Carl and Lucille Hamons bought the Provine Station in 1941 and renamed it Hamons' Court. When construction of Interstate 40 in the area was completed in 1962, access to Hamons' Court was cut off and the couple closed the motel. Carl passed away in 1971. Lucille eventually changed the station's name to Lucille's, and in 1997 it was placed on the National Register of Historic Places (as the Provine Station). In 1999, Lucille was inducted in the Route 66 Hall of Fame at age of 84. The original Hamons' Court sign was shipped to the Smithsonian Institute in 2003.

Lucille passed away in August 2000; hundreds attended her funeral. Anyone would be hard-pressed to accurately describe Lucille, who was at once kind and generous, but also stubborn and forceful when fighting for something she believed in. Countless times she provided food to hungry travelers with no money or a free place to stay when their cars broke down. She fought heartily for an exit when the Interstate threatened to cut off her business. When the state told her they were trying to get rid of these small places along the highway, it only fueled her resolve. She lived on Route 66 for 59 years, serving and caring for thousands along the way. She truly earned the title "Mother of the Mother Road."

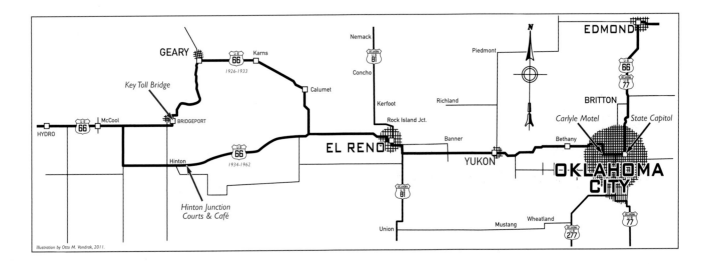

Illustration by Otto M. Vondrak, 2011.

WEATHERFORD, OKLAHOMA
c. 1952

On April 18, 1892, settlers began lining up at the western edge of Oklahoma's Cheyenne and Arapaho country in anticipation of the third Oklahoma land rush. One of these settlers, William J. Weatherford of Arkansas, settled his claim with his wife Lorinda, their four children, his widowed sister-in-law, and two hired hands. In an area that he called Jordan Flats, Weatherford built a five-bedroom house. In 1893 a post office was established in the house and Lorinda became its first postmistress.

In 1898 the Choctaw, Oklahoma & Gulf Railroad began its westward expansion and surprisingly located its terminus approximately 2 miles from the original Weatherford Settlement. On July 16, 1898, Beeks Erick, a local businessman, founded the location of current-day Weatherford and became town-site manager. Lots were sold and businesses, including a hotel and restaurant, were set up, albeit in tents. An application for a post office was sent to Washington, D.C., naming the new town Dewey, but the application came back stating there was already a town named Dewey in the territory. The post office at the Weatherford home was closed and the new town was named Weatherford.

Weatherford was incorporated on May 2, 1898, and Erick became the first mayor. Weatherford quickly became known as a rough and bawdy frontier town. As many as 20 saloons were said to operate within 60 days of its founding. By 1905 temperance groups had helped cut the number of saloons to two.

Regular train service began on November 14, 1898, and turned Weatherford into a major rail hub. Herds of cattle were regularly driven down Main Street to the railroad stockyards. In November 1926 that same dirt Main Street became U.S. Highway 66. By the 1960s much of Route 66 in the area was a four-lane highway, but in June 1970 exits and entrances to Interstate 40 were completed on either side of town and Weatherford became another victim of the dreaded Interstate bypass.

COTTON BOLL MOTEL, CANUTE
c. 1960

The small community of Canute is home to one of the most photographed landmarks on all of Route 66. The Cotton Boll Motel is certainly not the oldest motel on the route, nor is it an architectural standout, but something about the classic red and white sign outlined in red and green neon attracts tourists from around the country. Woodrow and Viola Penick, both former cotton farmers, built the Cotton Boll in 1960, using the classic L-shape with parking in front of each unit. A central courtyard was replaced with a swimming pool in later years. The back of this postcard advertises, "16 units completely new and modern. Wall to wall carpets. Tile baths, free TV in rooms. Refrigerated Air-conditioning, baby cribs, laundry, complimentary coffee in rooms."

Business was "excellent," according to Viola, until 1970 when Interstate 40 bypassed Canute. Woodrow and Viola sold the motel in 1979. During the short oil boom in the early 1980s the Cotton Boll's new owners rented rooms to workers from nearby oil fields. In the mid-1990s the motel was purchased by Pat and Cheryl Webb, who turned the office and Room 1 into a private home. To area residents, the Cotton Boll's sign has become a symbol and a reminder of the days when America's Main Street rolled through town. While many of these locals feared the new owners would have the sign removed, the Webbs have no intention of bringing down the landmark. "This is a big part of their life," Pat says.

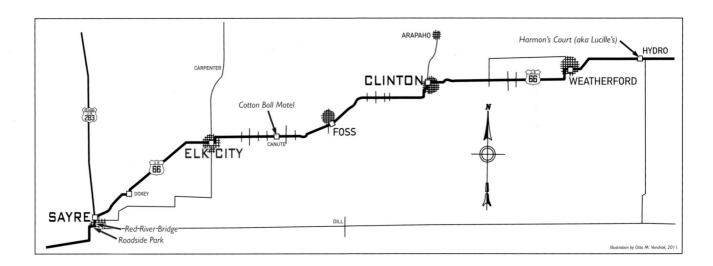

Illustration by Otto M. Vondrak, 2011.

ELK CITY
c. 1965

The path of Route 66 through western Oklahoma winds through several small towns and hamlets that once catered to the tourist trade. All of these towns have deep roots in the history of Route 66. Elk City is one such town.

Elk City became a town site in 1901. Its location at the western terminus of the Choctaw & Gulf Railway line turned Elk City into a major shipping center for the rail industry and became the major reason it grew as a city. Originally called Crowe, Elk City is believed to have taken its name from Elk Creek, which runs through town. Some say the town was once called Busch to lure Adolphus Busch into building a brewery in the area. The brewery never materialized, so the townspeople settled on Elk City.

Like many towns along Highway 66, including nearby Sayre, Elk City provided its own free tourist park. During the Great Depression, whether you stopped to rest, eat your lunch, or stay overnight, these parks were a welcomed sight to road-weary travelers. Originally called Ackley Park, Elk City's park is now known as City Park and is still a nice place to enjoy a picnic lunch.

In 1970, the interstate bypass was completed around Elk City. Down but not out, the townspeople got up, brushed themselves off, and got on with life after Route 66.

During the heyday of Route 66, Elk City was alive with motels, cafés, and service stations. Many of these vintage roadside businesses still exist today, hearkening back to the days when Route 66 was the primary artery that kept the nation on the go. Today, Elk City is the proud home of the National Route 66 Museum, reaffirming the town's deep 66 roots.

Route 66 crosses the pancake-like plains of the Texas panhandle, covering the 178 miles between Oklahoma and New Mexico. The panhandle is sometimes called the *Llano Estacado* or "Staked Plains," because early settlers in the area marked their routes by driving stakes into the ground. Kiowa and Comanche Indians roamed the region of Texas a mere 100 years ago.

People from all walks of life throughout the country saw Route 66 as a ticket to a new and better life "out West." During the late 1940s and into the 1950s families took to the road for their yearly vacations, often heading through Texas, which was fine as far as Texans were concerned. Route 66, which arrived in Texas in 1926, played an integral role in the economic growth of towns like Shamrock, McLean, Groom, Amarillo, Vega, and Adrain.

Early on, a journey through Texas on Route 66 was a rough, bumpy, and often hazardous ride. Because the Texas Highway Department gave priority to roads serving cities like Dallas, Houston, and San Antonio, conditions on 66 were generally subpar. One case in point was the dreaded "Jericho Gap," the portion stretching between McLean and Groom. After a rainfall many locals made extra cash by pulling stranded motorists out of the thick mud with teams of horses. In 1932 the section from McLean to Alanreed was bypassed and paved leaving about 18 miles of dirt from Alanreed to Groom. In 1933 construction finally began on a paved bypass there as well, but it wasn't until 1937 that the work was completed, making the stretch that paralleled the dreaded Jericho Gap one of the last sections on all of Route 66 to be paved.

During World War II military truck traffic took its toll on Route 66 in Texas, as it did in Missouri, and the surge of postwar automobile traffic further deteriorated the roadbed. Nevertheless, postwar families braved the road by the scores. Unlike its role in the 1920s and 1930s, Texas became a frontrunner in highway safety in the years following the war. Jack Rittenhouse, author of *A Guide Book to Highway 66* (1946), wrote when crossing the border from Oklahoma, "At once the road improves. Texas has wide splendid roads with excellent shoulders. There are many roadside parks throughout this part of the state." By 1954 Highway 66 was a modern four-lane highway from the Oklahoma border to just east of Groom, and from Amarillo west to Bushland. All of Route 66 in Texas was upgraded to four-lane status by 1960, with Interstate 40 designation from Shamrock to Conway. By 1966 the only two-lane section still in use was east of Vega to Glenrio at the New Mexico border. By the mid-1970s I-40 bypassed most Texas towns, with the exceptions of McLean and Groom. Amarillo, the largest Route 66 city in Texas, was completely bypassed in 1968. Groom survived the interstate until 1980, and McLean, one of the last holdouts along the entire route, did not succumb to I-40 until 1984.

Many of the towns that once enjoyed the abundance of postwar tourist travel have suffered the same sad fate as the road itself. During the road's heyday a trip west through Texas would include a multitude of "tourist traps." Live rattlesnake pits and great gas prices were but a few of the marketing ploys designed to convince travelers to stop. Some still exist but most have gone the way of the dial telephone. One holdover is the Big Texan Steak Ranch in Amarillo, which has a standing offer: finish their 72-ounce steak with all of the fixins' in one hour, and the meal is free.

U DROP INN, SHAMROCK
c. 1942

The art deco U Drop Inn at the intersection of Route 66 and U.S Highway 83 was built in 1936 from plans scratched out in the dirt by John Nunn with an old nail. So the story goes. The main building was built of brick with green and gold glazed tile accents, while the towers are wood-framed and covered with stucco. A contest to name the café was won by a local 10-year-old who pocketed $5 in the process. As the only café for about a 100-mile radius, the U Drop Inn enjoyed a brisk business.

Around 1937 the space next to the café that served as a store was transformed into a dining room and ballroom. Original proprietors John and Bebe Nunn sold the café after a few years, only to repurchase it in 1950 and change its name to Nunn's Café. John died in 1957, and in 1960 Bebe sold the business to Grace Brunner, who changed the name once again. The rechristened Tower Café also served as Shamrock's Greyhound bus station and fed hundreds of travelers daily. After a few more ownership changes, the building was purchased in the early 1980s by the son of the original financier, James Tindal Jr., who had the building repainted to its original color and restored the U Drop Inn moniker. Today the U Drop Inn is an information center created with a $1.7 million federal restoration grant.

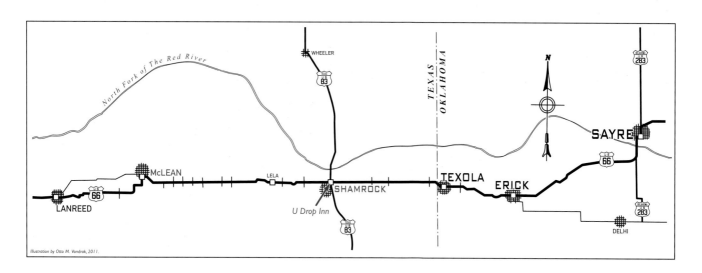

Illustration by Otto M. Vondrak, 2011.

SHAMROCK
c. 1960

At the far eastern edge of the Texas Panhandle, about 15 miles from the Oklahoma border, sits the town of Shamrock. The earliest white settlers in the area were mostly buffalo hunters bent on eradicating the vast herds with the blessing of the U.S. government. Because hunters draped bison hides over their makeshift homes, the area initially became known as Hidetown.

The postal service awarded Shamrock a post office in 1880. George Nickel, an Irish immigrant, was its first postmaster and named the region for his homeland. The railroads arrived in 1902 and formally brought civilization to Shamrock.

Early U.S. Highway 66 through the Texas Panhandle comprised mostly primitive dirt roads that twisted and turned through desert prairies. Conditions were so bad that the 90-mile trip from Shamrock to Amarillo in good weather was expected to take about two full days.

By the mid-1930s, Route 66 ran down Twelfth Street on the north side of town, and Shamrock began to grow like wildfire. In the later part of the decade, service stations, cafés, and auto courts sprang up everywhere along the strip, and in 1937 thousands attended a parade to celebrate the paving of Highway 66 through town. By the late 1960s, however, construction of the new interstate was progressing, and in 1972 the town of Shamrock was cut off by the new I-40.

Neon lights from the dozens of cafés, service stations, and auto courts once lit the evening skies and could be seen from as far as twenty miles away. Today, the "Little Las Vegas" strip is just a fading memory, and only a handful of businesses remain. Much of the neon and glitz along this stretch of highway has quietly faded into the emptiness of the Texas desert landscape.

McLean
c. 1962

McLean, Texas, began as a cattle-loading site for the Chicago-based Rock Island Railroad around 1902. English rancher, Alfred Rowe, whose vast ranch encompassed more than 200,000 acres of land in the region, donated the town site. In 1912, Alfred's fate was sealed when he booked passage on the maiden voyage of the *Titanic*.

The town was named McLean for Judge William Pinckley McLean, secretary of the first Texas Railroad Commission. In 1927, oil was discovered nearby and this sleepy little town began a rapid expansion. During World War II, a German prisoner-of-war camp was located east of town and was affectionately known as the "Fritz Ritz," with the first prisoners arriving in early 1943. The camp officially closed July 6, 1945.

The small town prospered and grew as a result of the U.S. Highway 66 commission in 1926. As many as 16 service stations, six motels, and numerous cafés lined Route 66 through town during the peak years of automobile travel. The Oklahoma-based Phillips Petroleum built its very first Texas-based service station in McLean in

1927. That station has been restored and is a favorite photo stop for tourists traveling on Old 66.

McLean was one of the last towns along the entire length of U.S. Highway 66 to see an interstate bypass. The townspeople fought the bypass as long as possible, but in March 1982, bypass construction began, and in the summer of 1984, Interstate 40 opened, leaving McLean to fend for itself. McLean suffered another substantial economic blow in the early 1980s when the Rock Island Railroad declared bankruptcy during the time the bypass took place. The town floundered but still manages to hang on as worldwide interest in historic Route 66 continues to attract an ever-increasing number of travelers through town. The Devil's Rope Museum complex located in town is dedicated to the history of barbed wire. The Texas Old Route 66 Museum and Western Heritage Community Room are also located within the complex and contain a wide variety of historic Route 66 exhibits as well as local historic displays.

GOLDEN SPREAD MOTEL, GROOM
c. 1953

In 1953, Pete Ford decided his next business venture would be in the motel industry. Already a success in ranching and oil, Ford bought up some vacant property in Groom and set out to build his motel. An architect based in Amarillo designed the motel but the unique arrow sign out front was Ford's own design. He built 22 rooms bordering a parking lot and called it the Golden Spread Motel, referring to the vast golden wheat fields throughout the Texas panhandle. The building on the west end of the complex housed the office while a second story above provided quarters for the manager.

The Golden Spread Motel was a member of the Best Western Motels chain and recommended by AAA. As competition increased, so did the need for motel owners to provide the latest in amenities. As with many other pool-less motels of the time, a heated swimming pool was added just steps from Route 66. After the interstate bypassed Groom in June 1980, the pool was removed. This decision was common, as the decline in business could no longer justify the expense of a pool.

In 1992, Steve Martin and company were shooting a film in Groom called *Leap of Faith*. The director wanted to use the Golden Spread in the movie, but the owner at the time declined the offer. The director liked the look of the motel so much that he found a motel on the west end of town, built a second story and sign to match the Golden Spread, and continued with the production. If you have ever driven through town and noticed a twin motel on the west side and wondered if there are two Golden Spread Motels in Groom, there is your answer.

Today the motel structure is currently used as the Route 66 Mini Storage.

GOLDEN SPREAD GRILL, GROOM
c. 1958

Groom is located 42 miles east of Amarillo. It was named for the first general manager of the Francklyn Land and Cattle Company, B. B. Groom, and laid out in 1902 on the route of the Rock Island Railroad. The 1920s brought an oil boom to the area, which, coupled with the new Highway 66, increased the town's population to 564 residents by 1931.

As oil production faded, agriculture and the tourist trade became the mainstays of the local economy. The Golden Spread Grill opened in 1957 and was one of four restaurants enjoying successful business in town. Soon after it opened, Ruby Denton took over the business and made the Golden Spread Grill a very popular eatery for travelers as well as locals. The back of the advertising postcard reads, "Always stop at the Golden Spread and be among the best fed." People did stop, and the restaurant's popularity grew.

Business boomed until one day in June 1980, when Interstate 40 bypassed Groom and crushed many of the town's roadside businesses. Today the structure that was once the Golden Spread Grill still stands and continues to serve travelers as the Route 66 Steakhouse.

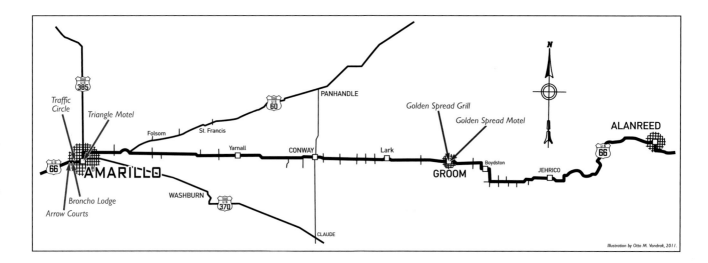

Illustration by Otto M. Vondrak, 2011.

TRIANGLE MOTEL, AMARILLO
c. 1949

S. M. Clayton was onetime mayor of Borger, Texas, known among some as "the wickedest town in the West." After his retirement from politics he and his wife Cora moved to Amarillo and built the Triangle Motel complex on the eastern edge of town, naming it for its wedge-shaped lot created by the intersection of Route 66 and Highway 60. The streamline moderne motel was designed with two parallel brick buildings that faced each other, separated by a courtyard in the center. Each building housed six rooms and a convenient, closed-in two-car garage between every two rooms.

During its heyday, the Triangle catered to the families and dependents of servicemen stationed at the nearby Lackland Air Force Base. In the late 1950s the Strategic Air Command opened the 4128th Strategic Wing at the base and extended its runways to accommodate the newer and bigger jets. Highway 60 was closed as a result. In 1968 the motel suffered two major setbacks with the deactivation of the air base and the completion of the Interstate bypass around Amarillo. Slowly, the motel fell into a state of disrepair. In 1977 Vaughn and Ramona Price bought the property and used the empty buildings mostly for storage. The structure that once housed the restaurant has since been opened and now serves as a bar and local hangout.

AMARILLO
c. 1958

In 1887 the Fort Worth & Denver City Railway was building across the Texas panhandle when it established a tent city, known as "Ragtown," along an area creek. A permanent townsite was subsequently argued over and voted on. On August 30, 1887, the site proposed by local rancher Colonel James T. Berry was selected. Originally called Oneida, it was soon changed to Amarillo (Spanish for "yellow"), some say for the color of the soil along the creek banks, others for the region's abundant yellow wildflowers. By 1893 it was said that Amarillo's population was "between 500-600 humans and 50,000 head of cattle."

In the early days, Route 66 entered Amarillo from the east via Northeast 8th Street (now Amarillo Boulevard) and continued just north of downtown, where it took a 90-degree turn south on Fillmore Street. The highway traveled through downtown, west on 6th Street, and on through San Jacinto Heights, veering off to 9th Street and eventually out of the city. Route 66 on 8th Street at the eastern end of town was considered "motel row," where dozens of tourist courts lined the street with colorful names like the Cowboy Motel, Cactus Motel, Silver Spur, Longhorn, and Wagon Wheel. By 1953 traffic was rerouted west on Amarillo Boulevard past Fillmore Street to relieve the traffic snarl downtown. The San Jacinto portion was paved in brick in 1927, making it the first paved highway in Amarillo. In 1968 Interstate 40 opened to traffic, bypassing the city and motel row.

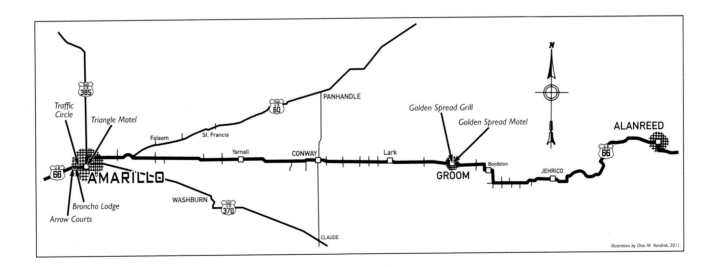

Illustration by Otto M. Vondrak, 2011.

TRAFFIC CIRCLE, AMARILLO
c. 1958

Route 66 through Amarillo has seen its fair share of changes over the years, including the original two-lane alignment that entered the city from the east being cut off by Amarillo's International Airport. In the fall of 1953, the original alignment through downtown and the San Jacinto District on Southwest 6th Street was bypassed when four-lane West Amarillo Boulevard was extended past Fillmore Street. Following the newer alignment west, Route 66 curved to the south, with the old and new alignments coming together at the intersection of Amarillo Boulevard and 9th Street. This intersection is simply called "the Circle" by locals and has to be one of the most convoluted and confusing intersections along the entire route. It's not what Cyrus Avery had in mind, I am sure.

Here, new four-lane 66, old two-lane 66 (9th Street), and Bell Street, as well as several exits, entrances, and an overpass carrying Bell Street, come together in what must look like a tangled piece of rope from above and which is just plain baffling at street level. I still get anxious every time I drive through the Circle, praying I don't get caught up in some sort of bizarre, nightmarish revolving door where

no matter how hard I try, I just can't seem to find the exit. A Route 66 version of *The Twilight Zone*.

The modern photo here was taken from the overpass. The old Veterans Hospital and water tower can be seen in the distance and give a great point of reference and perspective to the comparison.

BRONCHO LODGE, AMARILLO
c. 1951

Built in the early 1950s, the Broncho Lodge epitomizes the western-themed motels that proliferated alongside Route 66 from Amarillo westward. The motel is located on the west end of Amarillo near the intersection of old Route 66 (9th Street) and the newer four-lane Route 66 (now Amarillo Boulevard). From its beginning, the Broncho Lodge was considered a superior motel, evidenced by its AAA rating and Superior Seal of Excellence approval noted on the back of the postcard. The Broncho Lodge was heavily influenced by typical western ranch-style architecture. The motel's buildings form a U shape with the office centered at the front of the property. The original neon Broncho Lodge sign depicted a cowboy riding a bucking horse—a perfect image for the motel—but by the late 1950s, the original was replaced with a more contemporary-looking design.

The continued growth of auto travel in the 1950s translated into motel upgrades and the addition of modern amenities demanded by auto travelers. By the late 1950s, a café and steakhouse were added to the Broncho Lodge. Swimming pools were considered a motel standard by the early 1960s, and not having one ran the risk of losing business. The Broncho Lodge added a heated swimming pool in the late 1950s as well as a children's playground. Also added to the list of amenities was "free television." The canopies you see connecting the buildings were also a later upgrade, allowing customers to stay dry in the rain and out of the blazing Texas summer sun during check-in.

The Broncho Lodge continues operation today with 30 guest units, many of which are rented weekly.

BRONCHO LODGE
AMARILLO, TEXAS

ARROW COURTS, AMARILLO
c. 1955

By 1927 Amarillo was well on its way to becoming a popular tourist town. Motorists flocked into town via Highways 66, 60, 87, and 287—four major arteries that provided local roadside tourist stops with all the business they could handle. So great was the influx of visitors from the burgeoning auto/tourist trade that as many as 29 Amarillo auto courts and camps competed for the tourist dollar in 1927.

The Arrow Courts, later known as the Arrow Motel, were located on the western edge of greater Amarillo and were actually considered to be outside of the city limits. It was a good place to stop if you were traveling west and wanted to miss the city's morning traffic or the hustle and bustle of Amarillo's "Motel Row," located on the east side on Eighth Street. The Arrow's guest rooms were located in two buildings, one with four units and one with eight. An island courtyard filled with plants and trees lay parallel to the eight-unit building, forming a driveway with parking in front of each room. An office building located at the front of the property doubled as a gas station but provided no garage service. A café/restaurant unaffiliated with the motel was conveniently situated just west of the office. The Arrow Motel provided guests with panel-ray heat, carpeted floors, and tile baths. Owners and operators Mr. and Mrs. O. E. Allen (circa 1955) proclaimed the Arrow Motel to be "a clean, quiet place for a good night's rest."

In 1968 Interstate 40 bypassed the city and relegated Route 66 to I-40 business-loop status. In 1985, Highway 66 was decertified and left for dead. The Arrow Courts property is currently a private residence.

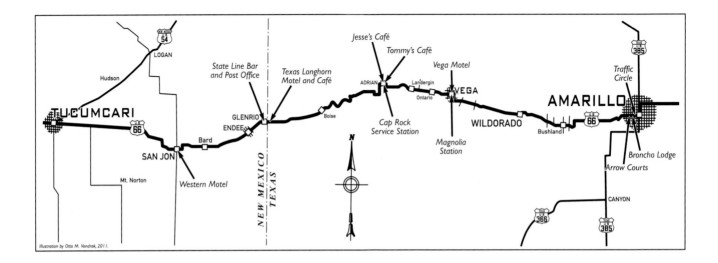

Illustration by Otto M. Vondrak, 2011.

VEGA
c. 1959

The small town of Vega, Texas, sits quietly along old Highway 66 about 30 miles west of Amarillo. Vega, Spanish for "grassy meadow," had its beginnings in 1897 when the state of Texas opened up the land in the area for homesteading. On October 17, 1899, early settler N. J. Whitfield purchased what would become the town site for $1 an acre. In May 1903 A. Miller and Howard Trigg surveyed the area, and Miller opened the first general store in Vega later that year. The following year a post office, saloon, and school were built, solidifying the fledgling community. A bank was established in 1908, and in 1909 the Choctaw, Oklahoma & Gulf Railroad (later the Rock Island) was completed, bolstering the town's economy. By 1915 Vega's population grew to 223.

Prior to 1926 the Old Ozark Trail carried the first automobile traffic through town. When Highway 66 was commissioned in 1926, the new highway followed along the original dirt pathway of the Ozark Trail through Vega. As automobile travel grew in popularity, tourist courts, service stations, and cafés were built all along the town's main street. By 1937 the highway was paved and realigned through town.

Vega was one of the last towns in Texas to see the Interstate 40 bypass, but by the late 1970s the inevitable was completed. Many early buildings still stand on both alignments of Route 66 through town, including the Magnolia Station, which dates to the early 1920s. The Vega Motel, an original tourist court, is also still in operation (see the first *Route 66 Lost & Found*).

Howdy from Vega, Texas

VEGA MOTEL, VEGA
c. 1960

In the small town of Vega, 40 miles west of Amarillo, sits the Vega Motel at the crossroads of old Route 66 and U.S. 385. E. M. and Josephine Pancoast built the 20-unit motel in the early 1940s, and it is a prime example of the era's U-shaped motor courts with a fully covered garage for each unit and a central courtyard. The property was sold to Ethridge Betts in the early 1970s, and the current owners, Harold and Tresa Whaley, bought the motel in 1988. Tresa sews the bedspreads and curtains used in the rooms. Many of the rooms have been remodeled, but Tresa says they are careful not to ruin the old charm and style. "Love, sweat and tears have gone into this place," says Tresa. When a blizzard left guests snowbound in 1991, Tresa's brother Manuel and daughter Joanna trekked to the grocery store in a four-wheel-drive vehicle. Tresa and Joanna then fixed a traditional Thanksgiving dinner for her family and stranded guests.

Unlike many owners of motels from this era, the Whaleys have not converted the garages to rooms, thus maintaining the 1940s styling. At the time of this writing, paperwork had begun to add the motel to the National Register of Historic Places. Tresa speaks fondly of the fact that in the early 1990s country music star Vince Gill shot the video for his song "I Never Knew Lonely" in Room 21.

MAGNOLIA STATION, VEGA
c. 1926

The Magnolia Station was built in 1924 by "Colonel" J. T. Owen on a lot he purchased in 1923, when the primitive dirt highway in front of it was known as the Ozark Trail. The Magnolia Station was the second service station built in Vega during the 1920s. By the time Highway 66 came through town, Edward and Cora Wilson had leased the Magnolia from Owen. The Wilsons lived above the station until 1930, when the Magnolia was leased to E. B. Cooke, who operated it for a short time before A. B. Landrum took over the lease in 1931.

In 1933 Owen's son Austin took over day-to-day operations at the station. He entered into a lease with the Phillips Petroleum Company, which charged him one cent per gallon of gasoline sold.

The highway directly in front of the Magnolia remained a dirt road during the time it served as Highway 66. By 1937 Route 66 was paved and realigned through Vega just south of the station, bypassing the downtown area. The Magnolia Station continued to provide gasoline until it shut down its pumps and ceased operation in 1953. The station was then used as a barbershop until 1965. It remained empty until the town of Vega and the Oldham County Chamber of Commerce restored it with partial funding from the Route 66 Corridor Preservation Program.

TOMMY'S CAFÉ, ADRIAN
c. 1962

Manuel Loveless built the Kozy Kottage Kamp in Adrian in the early 1940s. The Kamp's service station and café were destroyed by fire in December 1947, but the Loveless family continued renting cabins under the name Adrian Court. The property where the service station and café once stood was sold to the Harris family. Bob Harris, who had worked at the Kozy Kottage Kamp before World War II, returned after the war with the idea of building a café on the newly acquired property. Harris wanted to design the café in a way that would compel motorists to stop. The nearby U.S. Army Air Force bases were selling surplus military items, including a control tower. Harris bought the tower, moved it to his property, and proceeded to build his café around it. The eatery was christened the Bent Door Café for the canted door that accommodated its slanting walls.

Harris left Adrian and his mother to operate the café, and in 1950 Loveless leased the restaurant. In the late 1960s the Interstate bypassed Adrian and the steady flow of traffic slowed to a trickle. In 1970 the onetime 24-hour café and service station closed their doors. They sat empty for three decades until Harris returned for a visit and heard the café was to be condemned. He repurchased the property and set a reopening for September 9, 1995, but it wasn't to be. On September 9 the fryers and ovens sat empty and cold. The café has remained closed since.

JESSE'S CAFÉ, ADRIAN
c. 1965

In 1956 Dub Edmonds and former Navy cook Jesse Fincher opened Jesse's Café in "an old building a cowboy built of cinder blocks," recalls Edmonds. A gas station located alongside the café was also part of their enterprise, which at one time was a one-room, dirt-floor café called Zella's. In 1965 a second story A-frame apartment was added above the café and a new canopy was built over the pumps. The apartment burned twice and was not rebuilt after the second fire. Jesse's Café was so successful that a second restaurant, Jesse's #2, went up in nearby Wilderado about 30 miles east of Adrian. Edmonds and Fincher ran both locations until 1976 when they sold the Adrian location to Terry and Peggy Crietz, who

changed the name to Peggy's. The business was later sold again and became known as Rachel's.

Fincher's pies became famous in Adrian. Dub remembers, "He would bake pies and set them on the counter and most of them were sold before they got cold." Fincher passed away in 1989, leaving business matters to Edmonds, who sold the Wilderado location in 1991. Fran Hauser bought the Adrian location in 1990 and changed the name to the Adrian Café. Around 1995 she learned that Adrian was the mid-point on Route 66 and changed the name to the Mid-Point Café. Hauser continues the fine tradition of good food, friendly service, and delicious homemade pies begun in 1956.

CAP ROCK SERVICE STATION, ADRIAN
c. 1948

Percy Gruhlkey began operating the Cap Rock Service Station from a room in the front part of his home in the early to mid-1930s. From the beginning, Texaco gas flowed, first from gravity pumps then from modern electric pumps. The station was located about 5 miles west of Adrian and approximately 18 miles east of the town of Glenrio, which sits on the border of New Mexico and Texas.

Immediately after the war, Percy began building the cinder-block structure you see in the photo. This new building sat just a few yards west of his old station and home. Upon completion in about 1946, he moved the entire operation to this new building, which he painted white with a 24-inch green stripe running along the entire base of the structure. The words "Cap Rock Service Station" were painted over the door, also in green.

Percy's daughter Esther remembers that "the place was always busy." She also recalls, "The gas truck that brought our gas would sometimes have to come out here twice in a day, and we had 500-gallon storage tanks. That's how busy we were."

Esther remembers finally getting electricity when she was 12 or 13. Prior to that, one of her jobs was to make sure the wind generators charged the batteries that were used to run the pumps. At first an old 32-volt system was used for electrical needs, but as business picked up, the system was replaced and a 110-volt generator was installed.

The station was never open more than eight or nine hours a day, as Percy did not believe in killing oneself to make a buck. Not that he was lazy—on the contrary he was also busy with farming and carpentry. He did have a kind heart for people in trouble though. If a motorist ran out of gas after hours he would always make sure that they got the gas they needed, no matter the hour.

When the interstate came through the station closed, never to reopen. Percy Gruhlkey passed away in 1998.

TEXAS LONGHORN MOTEL, CAFÉ AND SERVICE STATION, GLENRIO
c. 1950

Scared away in 1946 by talk of a new interstate that was being built through Glenrio, local businessman Homer Ehresman and family packed their bags and moved to Plainview, Texas. As 1950 came around, this new interstate seemed to be stuck on the drawing table, so Ehresman, with family in tow, returned to Glenrio and built the Texas Longhorn Motel, Café and Service Station on the Texas side of town. The business ran smoothly until the Rock Island Railroad closed its depot in 1955, handing Glenrio a sharp economic blow.

But the knockout punch was still many years to come. Ehresman's business struggled for a period, but tourist traffic eventually flourished and the business grew. The Longhorn's iconic "First/Last Stop in Texas" sign grew from a simply painted board to a giant, illuminated billboard beckoning travelers to stop for a bite and spend the night. This enterprise remained highly successful for Ehresman until the dawn of the 1970s. The interstate that had been staved off for decades now spelled economic doom for Glenrio and its businesses. The enterprising Ehresman, down but not out, built a new, modern motel and restaurant just 5 miles west of Glenrio, on the north side of the interstate's Endee exit.

It is a bit ironic that the last few guests of Ehresman's Texas Longhorn Motel were the construction workers building his new motel. The First/Last Stop in Texas complex closed for good by 1975, and the "new" motel now lies in ruins. Glenrio, now a legitimate ghost town, sits quiet and alone. Route 66, its main street, once hectic and alive, has transformed into a tumbleweed highway with only a casual stray dog to interrupt the monotony. The towering beacon-like sign, once brightly lit and beckoning travelers, slowly crumbles with each passing year.

New Mexico was only 14 years old when Route 66 was created. The original 506-mile alignment through the state traversed many difficult obstacles, including deserts, snake-like canyons, and treacherous hills. Often the route utilized portions of the century-old Santa Fe Trail and the 300-year-old Camino Réal. The original alignment between Albuquerque and Santa Fe was considered the most treacherous and included the feared La Bajada Hill (Spanish for "the descent"). From 1926 to 1932 the hill provided early motorists with a multitude of challenges, including an average 6 percent grade and 20 switchbacks in 1.4 miles. Prior to the addition of fuel pumps in automobiles, motorists often climbed the hill in reverse to keep fuel flowing to gravity-fed carburetors. Descending La Bajada presented its own dangers. Early brake pads were often made of cloth and not very durable—riding one's brakes down the grade often set the pads on fire. At the top of the hill the State Highway Department posted a warning sign that read, "La Bajada Hill – Warning – Safe Speed 10 Mile – Watch Sharp Curves – This Road Is Not Fool Proof But Safe For A Sane Driver – Use Low Gear."

As automobiles gained popularity, many of the older paths traveled by Highway 66 quickly became obsolete. New Mexico saw its fair share of realignments, none as dramatic as that which took place in 1926. Around that time, Arthur T. Hannet was losing his bid for reelection as governor in a closely fought race. Feeling betrayed by his own political party and frustrated with state politics Hannet decided to avenge his loss by building a highway that would bypass the state capital. Governor-elect Richard Dillon would be sworn in in less than two months, so Hannet had little time to act. He called on state highway engineer E. B. Bail to begin a road-building project to start 6 miles west of Santa Rosa and head straight into Albuquerque. At the time, Highway 66 through New Mexico ran from Tucumcari to Santa Rosa, then to Romeroville, Glorieta, Santa Fe, and Albuquerque. Hannet's road would shorten the route to Albuquerque by about 89 miles and bypass Santa Fe's business community and politicians. By the time crews and equipment were secured, only 31 days remained to build 69 miles of roadway.

Angry citizens on Highway 66 to the north and Highway 60 to the south often sabotaged equipment, afraid of the economic impact of the new route. Vandalism, along with bitterly cold weather, slowed progress, but work forged ahead. Bail even brought the men blankets so they could sleep close to the machinery and protect it from further damage. Although the men worked non-stop, the new road was not quite finished by January 1. Dillon, immediately after taking oath on January 1, sent a representative to halt the construction. Bad weather kept him from arriving until January 3, however, by which time the road was completed. Hannet had his revenge. His road was originally designated New Mexico 6, paved by 1937, and redesignated as Highway 66 that same year.

The last segment of Route 66 in New Mexico was bypassed in 1981, four years before the entire route was officially decommissioned. In 1994 the surviving sections of Route 66 in New Mexico were designated as State Scenic Byways and in 2000 were recognized as National Scenic Byways.

STATE LINE
BAR/POST OFFICE, GLENRIO
c. 1943

Founded in 1903, two years after the Rock Island Railroad wound its way through the area, Glenrio quickly grew through the 1920s as an agricultural and farming community. The name Glenrio stems from the English word *glen* meaning "valley" and the Spanish word *rio* meaning "river," though Glenrio is neither in a valley nor near a river. Glenrio straddles the Texas–New Mexico border, but the post office is in New Mexico. This caused confusion early on, because the mail was delivered to a depot on the Texas side of town. Connected to the post office was the State Line Bar, which was operated on the New Mexico side of town because Deaf Smith County on the Texas side was dry. The fact that the post office and bar are connected makes one wonder if the mail was ever delivered on time.

Highway 66 was still a dirt pathway through town when Homer Ehresman and his wife, Margaret, first arrived in Glenrio around 1934. The Ehresmans quickly went into business operating a service station, bar, and tourist court, while Margaret also ran the post office. By the fall of 1937 the dirt pathway running through Glenrio was finally paved. During the construction that ran from summer to fall, workers camped in tents alongside the road. By 1946 talk of a new interstate that would bypass Glenrio prompted the Ehresman family to pull up stakes (see the Texas chapter).

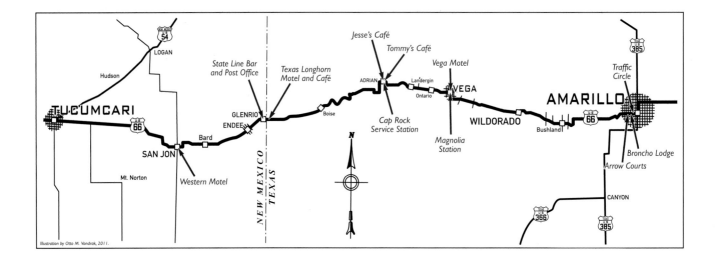

Illustration by Otto M. Vondrak, 2011.

Western Motel, San Jon
c. 1940

By 1969, Interstate 40 ran straight through from Oklahoma City west to Barstow with a few exceptions for small unfinished segments or bypasses that did not pose much of a problem for travelers. One exception to the exception was a segment of 20 miles or so in New Mexico. San Jon sits at the western terminus of this stretch while Glenrio anchors the eastern end of this once deadly segment. So hazardous was this stretch that it was commonly thought to be one of the deadliest stretches of roadway in all of New Mexico, referred to as "Death Alley" by New Mexico officials and truckers nationwide.

The Bureau of Public Roads' plan for the path of Interstate 40 to replace Death Alley would have placed San Jon some 5 miles south of the interstate. This move would have spelled certain doom for the small town. After a legal battle led by San Jon's former mayor, Earl Flint, the interstate was rerouted and San Jon was saved. Planning to completion took over six years, but by the summer of 1976, the segment from Tucumcari to Glenrio to San Jon was finished and San Jon got its off-ramp.

Which brings me to the Western Motel. After weeks of futile searching, I was unable to find out much on the hotel's history. What I could gather leads me to believe that the motel was built in the early 1940s. The back of the postcard reveals nothing except the postmark, which suggests the motel was in operation in October 1952. I have included it here because I have always been fascinated with the photo on the postcard, the tiny, lone office building seemingly just large enough for a small desk. It sure looks like the perfect backdrop for an Alfred Hitchcock suspense picture. The hand-painted sign purporting "Vacancy" and "Modern" leaning on a pole is another nice touch.

The Western Motel is just one of many places along Route 66 that has captured my imagination and piqued my curiosity over the years. It may wind up being one of those enigmatic, mysterious places along the road that may never reveal any of its history. Maybe it's better that way. A little mystery is good for the soul.

CACTUS MOTOR LODGE, TUCUMCARI
c. 1946

When I. E. and Edna Perry chose the location for the Cactus Motor Lodge on the east end of Tucumcari, they took into consideration that theirs would be the first motel travelers heading west would encounter. The Cactus Motor Lodge greeted its first guests in 1941.

The motel consisted of four buildings housing 25 guest units. Three of the buildings formed a U shape with the fourth building serving as a dance hall frequented by both locals and tourists. Each unit featured its own private, lockable, and fully enclosed garage, as well as free radio and double insulated walls.

In 1952, Edna sold the Cactus Motor Lodge to Norm and Irene Wegner. In an effort to modernize the motel's appearance, the Wegners had an artificial stone applied to the exterior of all four buildings. The Wegners also converted the dance hall to a manager's residence and office. The Wegners operated the motel for 20 years until their retirement in 1972 when the business was sold to Harry and Jean Schiermeyer. In May 1976, the Cactus Motor Lodge changed

hands again and was sold to Frank and Elizabeth Kocab. Finally, in 1979, Andy and Sugandhi Patel purchased the motel and continue to operate the business to this day.

The interstate bypassed Tucumcari in the early 1980s, and travelers no longer had to drive Route 66 through town. This change put a major squeeze on most local businesses, and the Cactus Motor Lodge was no exception. By the 1990s, business was so bad that the motel units were closed and the 1960s-era swimming pool was removed. The courtyard was converted to an RV park.

In March 2006, the Cactus Motor Lodge was listed on the National Register of Historic Places. Early in 2007, the New Mexico Route 66 Association, with funding provided by the National Park Service Route 66 Corridor Preservation Office, began restoration of the Cactus Motor Lodge sign, including the addition of new neon, replacement of the sheet-metal shrouding around the sign poles, and replication of the stone base. Today, the restored sign proudly fronts the motel, beckoning travelers with its newly found glow.

BLUE SWALLOW COURT, TUCUMCARI, NEW MEXICO

In the City, East on U. S. Highway 66

BLUE SWALLOW COURT, TUCUMCARI
c. 1941

Since the early 1940s, the Blue Swallow has been a favorite haven among weary travelers. W. A. Huggins began construction on this truly classic motor court in 1939 and opened for business in 1941. The archetypal 1930s design features 13 units laid out in an L-shape with individual garages for each unit. The office sits prominently in the center. Ownership changed hands a few times over the years until 1958 when Floyd Redman purchased the property and gave it to his fiancée as an engagement gift. Lillian Redman owned and operated the motel for almost 40 years until age and the high cost of upkeep took their toll.

Slowly, the motel was headed downhill from lack of maintenance and Redman was forced to put it up for sale. With no prospective buyers it seemed another Route 66 icon was about to fade away. Fortunately, Dale and Linda Bakke saw an ad in a Denver newspaper listing the Blue Swallow for sale and, looking for a change of scenery, purchased the property. On March 13, 1998, substantial restoration efforts began. Unit by unit, room by room, and fixture by fixture, the classic Blue Swallow was lifted from the brink of extinction. Lillian Redman passed away in February of 1999 but no doubt would smile as once again the Blue Swallow proudly serves tired travelers.

TUCUMCARI
c. 1957

Tucumcari (pronounced *too-come-carry*) was first christened Six Gun Siding, but in 1902 citizens agreed that a more "respectful" name was needed, so they named it after a nearby mountain. Legend has it that a chief ordered two competing braves to the top of the mountain to fight to the death for the honor of marrying his daughter, Kari. Her lover, Tocom, lost the battle and in a violent rage she killed the victorious brave. Filled with anguish, she then sunk Tocom's knife into her own heart. Upon seeing what had transpired, the chief took the knife and plunged it into his own heart. Use your imagination, adjust the spelling a little, and voila.

During the halcyon days of Route 66, the indelible words "Tucumcari Tonight! 2,000 Motel Rooms" were splattered across billboards from Oklahoma City to California. Tucumcari was known as the town that was "two blocks wide and two miles long," for the concentration of motels, service stations, trading posts, and cafés along Route 66 through town. In the early days, however, Route 66 from the Texas border to Tucumcari was not well maintained and extremely narrow. Old timers would remark that you had "six inches and a cigarette paper between you and death on 66." Interstate 40 bypassed Tucumcari in 1980, but the town managed to survive. There may be fewer motel rooms these days, but the main drag is still filled with historic Route 66 motels, cafés, trading posts, and a legend or two for good measure.

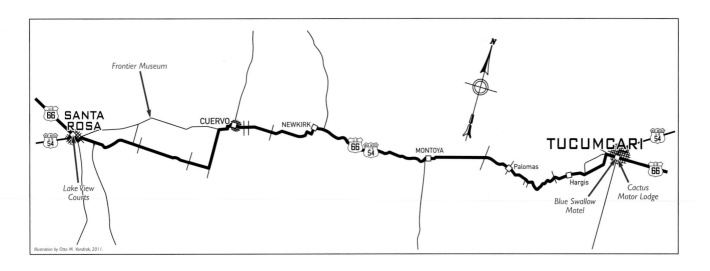

Illustration by Otto M. Vondrak, 2011.

Frontier Museum Santa Rosa, New Mexico

FRONTIER MUSEUM, SANTA ROSA
c. 1954

The final routing of Route 66 from Cuervo to Santa Rosa was completed in the early 1950s. That alignment today is mostly covered under the path of current I-40. Located about 9 miles east of Santa Rosa, the Frontier Museum was opened around 1954, soon after the new routing was completed. The complex was built by local contractor Max Rivera for W. S. Wilson and consisted of a service station, bar, café, museum, and curio shop. The museum contained hundreds of

native and western relics from the area. A pair of bison was even kept in back of the museum and became favorites among tourists.

Although the Frontier Museum has an exit, the interstate and changing popularity of auto travel doomed the western-themed roadside business. By the early 1980s, the Frontier Museum was closed and all of the artifacts and most of the café kitchen equipment were auctioned off, including the magnificent all-wood

bar that saw its share of beers served up to thirsty travelers.

The Frontier Museum came to life again in the mid-1980s when Robert Rivera, the son of the original contractor, purchased the property. By the time Rivera bought the property around 1985, the place was in total disrepair. Rivera proceeded to remodel the inside of the building with his sights on reopening the property as a bar and dance club. He gutted the inside and built a stage for bands.

The bar was simply called The Frontier and catered mostly to local clientele. The Frontier carried on for five or six years and closed its doors around 1993. The building stood empty for 10 years prior to being destroyed by fire around 2003. Today the deteriorating ruins of the vintage Frontier Museum sit on the side of the modern interstate, offering, for a brief moment, a compelling picture of roadside cultures past and present.

LAKE VIEW COURTS, SANTA ROSA
c. 1946

The Lake View Courts were built in 1941 and consisted of 10 units with covered garage parking for four of the rooms. A station serving Conoco gas was also part of the original structure. The motel operated as a successful business for 20 years until the early 1960s when the owner allowed it to fall into a state of disrepair. In the mid-1960s Canuto Sanchez Jr. purchased the property with the intent of tearing the motel down and erecting a new modern Ramada Inn in its place. Canuto decided against the new motel when news that the impending Interstate would eventually bypass Santa Rosa was confirmed. He opted to spruce up the existing motel with some fresh paint and to furnish the rooms with new beds and furniture. Along with the new look came a new name and the Lake View Courts were changed to the Plains Motel. The newly remodeled inn and newly added Amoco gas station became favorite stops in town until November 1972 when the Interstate was completed, leaving Santa Rosa high and dry. The motel closed in April 1973 and has been used for storage for the past 30 years. The service station reopened in 1975 under the Exxon banner and remained open until 1980.

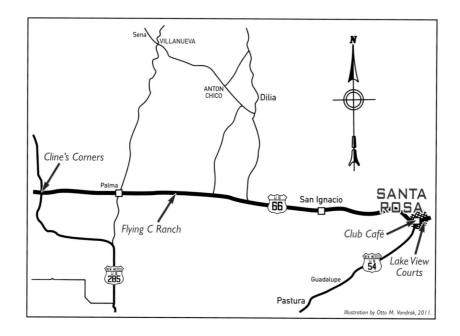

Illustration by Otto M. Vondrak, 2011.

SANTA ROSA
c. 1958

Santa Rosa, was founded in 1865 when rancher Don Celso Baca, drawn by the abundance of water, arrived and became "lord of the region" under the old custom of range domain. He named the new settlement after his wife and Saint Rose of Lima, the first canonized saint of the so-called New World. The coming of the railroad on Christmas Day 1901 turned the sleepy settlement into a vital transportation and service hub. Ironically, water, which attracted the railroad, was also the reason that industry fled Santa Rosa: the water was so high in mineral content it left gypsum deposits in steam engines, ruining the locomotives. With the departure of the railroad, Santa Rosa reverted to the sleepy town it once was.

When Highway 66 was routed through in 1926, Santa Rosa became an important stop. At one time, as many as 60 service stations, 20 motels, and 15 restaurants lined its main thoroughfare. The famous Blue Hole, located on one of Route 66's early alignments through town, is a natural, bell-shaped pool over 80 feet deep with amazing clarity and a constant water temperature of 64 degrees Fahrenheit. Scuba divers from around the country enjoy its unique blue waters. During the Dust Bowl era, the Blue Hole and the surrounding area served as a campground for thousands of migrants.

CLUB CAFÉ, SANTA ROSA
c. 1955

If you drove anywhere near Route 66 in the Southwest during its heyday, you were sure to see one of the billboards depicting the Club Café's jolly, smiling, fat man. The eatery's front man was one of the most endearing logos to make its way to a billboard during the Mother Road's halcyon days.

The Club Café got its start in 1935 when Floyd Shaw and Phil Craig operated a small 24-seat café in Santa Rosa. Floyd was working on Route 66 as a highway surveyor at the time for the road's new path to Albuquerque. Although popular at the time, the café's early success was just a harbinger of the things to come.

The year 1937 saw the new path of Route 66 completed. No longer did the road go through Santa Rosa then jog north to Santa Fe and down to Albuquerque. Route 66 now traveled through Santa Rosa and headed straight on through to Albuquerque. People began stopping at the café in record numbers. The partners sold the small café and opened a new, larger facility to accommodate the large crowds. Floyd and Phil began erecting billboards all over the Southwest depicting the café's smiling fat man mascot. Phil was responsible for the original artwork, and some speculate that the image is taken from his own likeness. The café became known nationwide as word quickly spread among truckers and travelers

about the Club Café's excellent food and service. The specialty of the house was sourdough biscuits and Pinto beans.

The Club Café enjoyed success throughout the 1940s, '50s, and '60s until the interstate came through in 1972, cutting the town in half and leaving the Club Café stranded and far from an off-ramp. In 1973, former employee Ron Chavez, returning from work in California, witnessed the terrible state that both the town and café were in. He went on to purchase the café and proceeded to build the business back to its former glory. The newfound success ended in 1992 when the Club Café served its last meal. A recession and too much fast food competition were given as the causes of the café's demise.

In 1995, Jose A. Campos purchased the Club Café building with a vision to reopen the eatery. His family had owned and operated Joseph's Restaurant in town since 1956 and thought it would be a great idea to reintroduce the fat man. Unfortunately the building was not up to code and so far gone that reopening it as a restaurant was not feasible. Today, after purchasing the rights to the smiling fat man logo, the Campos family has at least given new life to the former iconic Club Café mascot. The smiling fat man lives on, greeting a new generation of hungry patrons at Joseph's Restaurant. He looks happier than ever with his new job and employer.

FLYING C RANCH, PALMA
c. 1945

Located 77 miles east of Albuquerque, near a speck of a town called Palma, the Flying C Ranch was built in 1945 by Roy Cline, who is more widely known for establishing Cline's Corners in 1933. In 1939 Cline sold the very successful Cline's Corners and moved on to Kingman, Arizona. After a few additional pit stops, he returned once again to eastern New Mexico, where he built the Flying C Ranch.

The Flying C Ranch featured a garage complete with wrecker, a filling station selling Texaco gas, and a small café. Much of the Flying C Ranch's business came from stranded motorists unaccustomed to traveling the Southwest's desert during the hot summer months. After completing a few stucco repairs, Cline's son painted one of the buildings stark white. The color attracted customers, and soon all the buildings were painted white. The Flying C developed into an all-purpose travel center when it became a regular stop for the Greyhound bus line.

Cline owned and operated the Flying C Ranch until 1963. Both Cline's Corners and the Flying C Ranch remain in business today without the involvement of any Cline family members. The Flying C is currently owned and operated by Bowlin Travel Centers Incorporated. The Bowlins have been meeting the needs of the traveling public since 1912, when Claude M. Bowlin began trading with Native Americans of New Mexico. The Bowlins currently own and operate 12 travel centers, all located in the Southwest, three of them on Historic Route 66. Each full-service travel center offers gifts, souvenirs, exclusive handmade Indian jewelry, and gasoline. Many also feature Dairy Queen restaurants. In 1972 Bowlin's youngest son, Michael L. Bowlin, became president and CEO of the operation and remains in charge to this day. Claude M. Bowlin died in 1974.

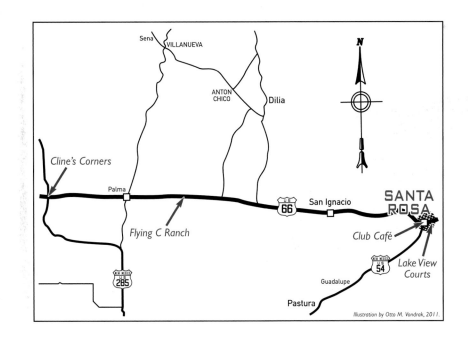

Illustration by Otto M. Vondrak, 2011.

CLINE'S CORNERS
c. 1958

After several failed business ventures in New Mexico and Arkansas, Roy Cline and his son Roy Jr. in 1934 leased 80 acres where Highways 6 and 2 intersected and built a small café and Conoco station. In 1937 the highways were paved and relocated, so Roy had the buildings jacked up and moved to the new intersection, Highway 2 now being U.S. Highway 285 and Highway 6 becoming Route 66. During the early years, things were tough going. At night Roy turned on the lights only when a car approached. If they stopped he left them on; if they passed, he turned them off and waited for another car.

Eventually, Cline's Corners became Roy's most lucrative venture. He sold the business in 1939 and moved, but eventually returned to New Mexico and opened another Route 66 service station, which he owned and operated until 1963. Located 77 miles east of Albuquerque, the Flying C Ranch at first consisted of a gas station, garage, and café. Today, it is a fully modern facility known as Bowlin's Flying C Ranch, and includes a gas station, curio shop, and Dairy Queen. After Roy sold Cline's Corners, it became so large that in 1964 a post office was added and homes were built behind the business to provide living quarters for most of its 48 employees. Over the years Cline's Corners became a Route 66 landmark and, later, a favorite stop on Interstate 40 that today serves an estimated 15 million customers each year.

CLINES CORNERS
At the Overpass Where U. S. 285 Meets U. S. 66
New Mexico's Most Popular Highway Stopping Place
CAFE, CURIO SHOP AND SERVICE STATION

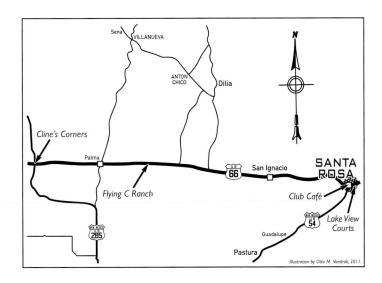

Illustration by Otto M. Vondrak, 2011.

LONGHORN RANCH, MORIARTY
c. 1948

"Where the West Stops to Rest" was the catchy advertising slogan of the Longhorn Ranch. Located 45 miles east of Albuquerque, the Longhorn sat along Route 66 on the barren desert landscape of eastern New Mexico, tempting first-time travelers out West to stop and rest a spell. "Captain Eric" Erikson, a former police officer from back East, opened the Longhorn with only a counter and a few stools. Eventually the tiny café was expanded to include a restaurant, coffee shop, cocktail lounge, motel, curio shop, and full-service garage. The storefronts were set up to look like the Western towns one would see in the movies, with a pair of totem poles guarding the curio shop.

The Longhorn was the first taste of the Old West for many motorists traveling along Route 66. Among the many attractions at the ranch, riding the bright red stagecoach, pulled by four paint horses with Hondo the Cowboy at the reins, was probably the most popular. Afterward, kids could have their picture taken with Hondo and the stagecoach. The Longhorn Ranch also kept several exotic animals on display for tourists to enjoy, including oxen, a large Brahma bull, buffalo, and a special longhorn steer named "Babe." The Longhorn Ranch became a landmark institution on Route 66, and at its height of popularity hosted thousands of tourists each day. Today, only ruins and memories remain of one of the most glamorous tourist attractions on Route 66.

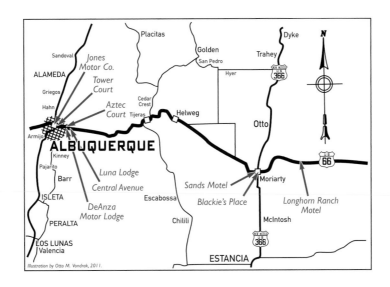

Illustration by Otto M. Vondrak, 2011.

LONGHORN RANCH MOTEL, MORIARTY
c. 1950

Located 70 miles west of Santa Rosa, the Longhorn Ranch Motel was a later addition to the landmark Longhorn Ranch complex. The Longhorn Ranch was built by one-time police officer Captain Eric Erickson, who began his business as a café with a few stools and a single counter. The wide-open desert between Santa Rosa and Albuquerque was barren and often harsh, with few tourist facilities along the way—the perfect scenario for the successes of tourist meccas like Cline's Corners, the Flying C Ranch, and the Longhorn Ranch. After World War II these outpost businesses expanded like wildfire. The Longhorn Ranch soon became an institution on Route 66, and travelers made it a point to stop there year after year.

At its peak the Longhorn Ranch included a café, garage, service station, curio shop, museum, cocktail lounge, restaurant, and motel. The motel was built on the north side of Highway 66, directly across from the main complex. It featured 15 ranch-style units and an office built to resemble a Western ranch house. The ranch-type setting was the perfect complement to the Old West theme that permeated the main complex across the highway. According to the period postcard, a night's rest at the Longhorn Ranch Motel was "air cooled by Nature" and offered rubber-foam mattresses and a café just "across the highway with one of the finest Dining Rooms and Cocktail Lounges on Highway 66."

Nothing but memories remain of the main Longhorn Ranch complex. So thorough was the demolition that one would be hard-pressed to even prove that the landmark roadside stop ever existed. The motel units survive, however, and provide a small taste of what a visit to one of the largest and most glamorous tourist facilities on Route 66 was like. If you decide to stop at the motel, take some time and walk across the old highway to the one-time site of the main Longhorn Ranch complex. If you stand very still, you might hear the sound of the ranch's famous Concord stagecoach whizzing by as Hondo the driver barks out orders to his team of horses.

BLACKIE'S PLACE, MORIARTY
c. 1949

During a stint as a Greyhound bus operator, Herbert Odell Ingram (a.k.a. Blackie) had a regular stop in the town of Buford (now Moriarty) at the Thunderbird Café. (Moriarty was incorporated in 1953.) As a result of his layovers in town, he became friends with the owner of the Thunderbird Café, and in 1944, when the café came up for lease, Blackie (so-called for the color of his hair), knowing a good opportunity when he saw it, seized the moment and signed the lease. The business took off and before a year was up Blackie found himself looking for his own place.

Blackie's Place opened in 1945 and consisted of a café and a Sinclair gas station. That same year, he married Norma Danielson, a waitress he hired to work at the Thunderbird. Blackie's Place quickly became a 24-hour tourist center when the Greyhound stop was officially moved there from the Thunderbird Café. Blackie built an addition to the east end of his café in 1949. This new space was crammed with curios and souvenirs of all types and was called Golden Eagle Traders.

Blackie knew the value of advertising. His billboard campaign ran east from Oklahoma City and stretched as far west as Seligman, Arizona. Just plain, simple, black-and-yellow billboards with the words "Blackie's Place" and a mileage count—just enough to pique one's curiosity.

Hubert Odell Ingram passed away in 1966, but through the efforts of his widow, Blackie's Place continued operation. Norma sold the business in 1975, at which time Blackie's turned from a café into a bar. Blackie's changed hands again when J. T. Turner, owner of the Tomahawk Trading Post, took over. J. T. eventually sold to the current owner who runs a pharmacy on the property. The Blackie's name reappeared in 2004 when Dell Kemper opened Blackie's Bar and Grill a few yards west of the old building.

AZTEC COURT, ALBUQUERQUE
c. 1941

In 1931 Guy and May Fargo built the Aztec Court at an estimated cost of $8,000 at 3821 Central Avenue on the east side of Albuquerque. "Innerspring mattresses, furnace heat and moderate rates" were some of the advertised amenities. In 1937 Route 66 was relocated to New Mexico 6, a straight shot from Santa Rosa to Albuquerque, giving Central Avenue a major increase in traffic. Tourist-based businesses began popping up all along the street, as a steady stream of automobiles flowed down Route 66, especially in the summer months. Guy passed away in 1942 but May continued to operate the motel until she sold it in 1944. Two years later the property was again sold to a pair of couples, William and Emma Geck and

Wesley and Bertha Meyer, who owned and operated the motel until the early 1950s. Later in the decade the name was changed several more times through the course of eight ownership changes. In 1958 Floyd and Evelyn Lewis bought the property and changed the name to Aztec Motel, which remains in use today. The Aztec passed through a few more hands between 1962 and 1992, when Mohamed and Shokey Natha bought the property. After 64 years and 14 ownership changes, the oldest continuously operated auto court on New Mexico's Route 66 was entered into the National Register of Historic Places in 1993. Nevertheless, demolition of the motel began in June 2011.

JONES MOTOR COMPANY, ALBUQUERQUE
c. 1943

In 1939 Ralph Jones built the Tom Danahy–designed structure that housed the Jones Motor Company. Hoping to meet the needs of the modern auto owner and traveler, Jones later incorporated a Texaco gas station, creating a Ford dealership and repair center all under one roof. Sitting on a prime location on the east side of town, the auto-repair station was one of the first encountered by westbound travelers on Highway 66.

One of the most notable characteristics of the Streamline Moderne–style building is the stepped tower, which is adorned with ornamental molding that underscores the tower's shape. The tower was centrally located over the main portion of the building and housed the service station's restrooms. In 1946 an additional showroom was added to the west side of the building to mirror the original showroom. During the 1950s, a paint and body shop was added in a separate structure to the south of the gas station.

During the Jones Motor Company's early years, many of the repairs done were on vehicles being driven out West by people fleeing the Dust Bowl. These vehicles were so loaded down with family possessions that access to broken parts was difficult at best. Jones built a long carport along the southern wall of the garage so that cars and trucks could be unloaded in the shade, thus making the vehicles more accessible for repair.

Jones was born on a cattle ranch in Wyoming, where he spent most of his early years. At the end of World War I cattle prices began to plummet, and, desperately needing to supplement his income, Jones took a job selling Model T Fords in Cheyenne. In 1928 he opened his first Ford dealership in Springer, New Mexico. That dealership was eventually moved to the Central Avenue location in Albuquerque and reopened as the Jones Motor Company.

Jones was a huge advocate of Highway 66 and was onetime president of the Route 66 Association, as well as president of the Albuquerque Chamber of Commerce and chairman of the New Mexico State Highway Department during the mid- and late 1940s. The business moved in 1957, and in the subsequent decades the building changed hands several times. The structure housed several businesses, including an army surplus store, a paint and body shop, and a moped dealership. In 1993 the Jones Motor Company building was listed on the National Register of Historic Places. In 1999 it was purchased by Dennis and Janice Bonfantine and lovingly brought back to life as a brewpub and restaurant called Kelley's Brewery. Great efforts were made to return the structure to its original design, including the preservation of the vintage garage doors and the addition of two classic Texaco gas pumps out front.

CENTRAL AVENUE, ALBUQUERQUE
c. 1950

The Spanish villa of Albuquerque was founded in 1706 on the banks of the Rio Grande by Don Francisco y Valdes, the governor of New Mexico. The villa was named for the Duke of Alburquerque, the viceroy of New Spain, and as a result is sometimes referred to as the "Duke City." (The first *r* in Alburquerque was eventually dropped.) A vital stop on the *El Camino Real* or "King's Highway" connecting Mexico City to Santa Fe, the settlement grew quickly. In 1879 the Atchison, Topeka & Santa Fe Railway steamed into the area and established New Albuquerque about 1 1/2 miles east of what is now called Old Town. The following year, on April 22, the first rail passengers pulled into the new boomtown.

When Highway 66 was designated in 1926, the road passed through town via Fourth Street, crossed the Barelas Bridge, and continued down Isleta Boulevard. In 1937 the Santa Fe Loop was bypassed, and Route 66 traveled into town via Central Avenue.

Prior to realignment in 1935, only 3 tourist camps were located on Central Avenue, while 16 were in operation on Fourth Street. Four years after the realignment, Central Avenue became the focus of tourist facilities. Roadside development flourished, and the number of motels increased to 37.

After World War II and the end of gasoline rationing, the country once again looked to the automobile for vacation travel. By 1955, 98 motels were located on Route 66 within the city limits of Albuquerque. The vintage buildings and motels along the older Fourth Street alignment and the newer Central Avenue alignment represent a virtual museum of popular architectural styles utilized during Route 66's heyday out West, from Pueblo Revival to Southwest vernacular to Streamline Moderne. Of the 98 motels operating along Central Avenue during Route 66's peak years, about 40 that date prior to 1955 still exist today. In 1970 Albuquerque was entirely bypassed by Interstate 40.

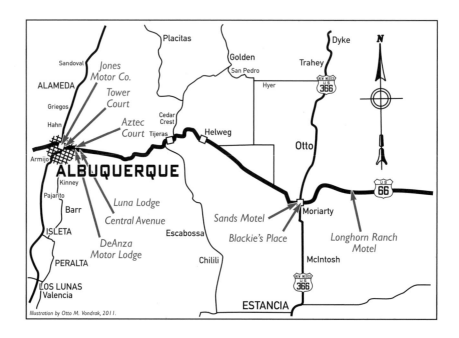

Illustration by Otto M. Vondrak, 2011.

WEST CENTRAL AVE.
ALBUQUERQUE, NEW MEXICO

TOWER COURT, ALBUQUERQUE
c. 1939

The Tower Court was built by Ben F. Shear in 1939, just two years after the relocation of Route 66 through Albuquerque via Central Avenue. The mostly single-story motel was constructed using the classic U-shape layout and utilizes a distinctively streamline moderne architectural style. Typical of auto court design during the 1930s, pull-in garages were located alongside each unit, with all but one still in use today. The unusual rear wing of the motel contains a second story consisting of two units mirroring the lower units. Originally, a 30-foot stepped tower containing the motel office was located at the front of the property, accentuating the unique design of the motel. The tower has since been removed. The motel was originally built containing 15 units and remained that way with no additions over its lifetime. The Tower Court was a member of the United Auto Courts and was a recommended stop by AAA. Eventually, to keep up with the times, the "Court" was dropped and the name was changed to the Tower Motel. Relatively unchanged since 1939, the Tower Motel is one of the oldest remaining tourist courts along Albuquerque's Central Avenue/Route 66 commercial strip. It is also a classic example of auto courts built prior to World War II. The Tower Motel no longer serves nightly guests but is an apartment building renting units by the month. On November 22, 1993, it was added to the National Register of Historic Places.

El Vado Court, Albuquerque
c. 1937

In anticipation of Route 66 being rerouted through Albuquerque, Dan Murphy set out to build his motor court. Murphy reportedly learned the business from working as a bellboy at the Waldorf-Astoria in New York and at the Franciscan in Albuquerque.

The year 1937 saw scores of tourist businesses built along Central Avenue. These motor courts, gas stations, and restaurants would eventually line Central Avenue for most of its entire length through town. At night the neon glow from these businesses lit up the nighttime sky and turned Central Avenue into an explosion of color. Motels were being built at an astonishing rate, and by 1955, motels located on Central Avenue reached a high of 98.

The El Vado is situated just west of the Rio Grande on the south side of Route 66. It was built on 1.26 acres with two parallel rows of buildings facing a common parking area and housing a total of 32 rooms. The office was located at the front of the building on the east end. The motel was built in the Spanish pueblo revival style, a common architectural style found on structures all along Central Avenue.

Tourists staying at the El Vado were treated to soundproof and fireproof rooms. A nearby "bathing beach" on the Rio Grande, now called Tingley Beach, and an adjoining public golf course were but a few of the perks offered to guests. A swimming pool was added but has since been filled in. The classic neon Indianhead sign out front was not part of the original design but was added at a later date, as is evident by the word "Motel" used in the sign as opposed to "Court."

In 2005, owner Sam Kassam sold the property, citing lack of business. Richard Gonzales bought the motel and property for the sole purpose of developing a condominium complex on the site. Since his purchase, a ferocious battle has raged to save the landmark motel and keep it from being razed. The mayor of Albuquerque even joined the fight by applying for city landmark status for the motel, a move approved by the city council in February 2006 but overturned by the state district court after Gonzales appealed the decision. As of this writing the legal battle to save the El Vado continues.

The El Vado was listed on the National Register of Historic Places and the State Register of Cultural Properties in 1993.

ARROW-HEAD CAMP, GLORIETA
c. 1926

The Arrow-Head Camp was located 22 miles east of Santa Fe on the original alignment of old Highway 66. The road through this area follows the path of the old Santa Fe Trail and is rich with wonderfully historic tales of the Old West. Here the Santa Fe Trail eventually developed into the National Old Trails Highway, Highway 66, and, presently, New Mexico Highway 50. The ancient road in front of the Arrow-Head Camp has seen the gamut of transportation over the last 150 years or so, from horse and wagon to big rigs.

The Arrow-Head Camp was quite a large facility for its time and included a store, cabins, campground, and gas station. During the 1930s the cost for an overnight stay in one of the cabins was 50 cents. Later in the 1940s, the Arrow-Head Camp became known as Arrowhead Lodge and was a popular spot among locals for dinner and dancing. The camp, which comprised mostly log cabin structures, was also a favorite among tourists and sportsmen, situated as it was in a highly wooded, picturesque area.

Route 66's Santa Fe Loop through Glorieta saw service from November 11, 1926, until January 1937, when a new routing of the road straight from Santa Rosa to Albuquerque shaved off about 90 miles of New Mexico Route 66 roadway. Today the wooded setting that made the camp so scenic is slowly overtaking the log structures. Long ago the Arrow-Head Camp began the process of blending in with the neighboring trees and brush. One day, the camp will complete its journey and totally succumb to its surroundings.

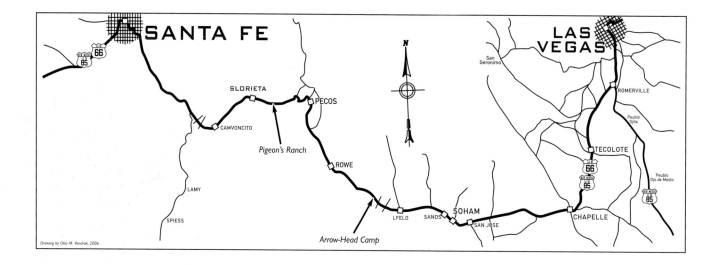

PIGEON'S RANCH, GLORIETA
c. 1929

Frenchman Alexander Valle built Pigeon's Ranch in the early 1820s, around the time that the Santa Fe Trail was being blazed. The name came from the fact that Valle spoke "pigeon English," or broken English, with a heavy French accent. The ranch became a very important site along the Santa Fe Trail, serving as a stagecoach stop, U.S. post office, and trading post.

On March 28, 1862, Pigeon's Ranch and the surrounding area, known as Glorieta Pass, was the site of the biggest and bloodiest battle of the Civil War in the Southwest. The adobe building shown here is said to have been used as a field hospital during that battle.

In 1924 Thomas "Tommie" Greer acquired the ranch and turned it into a roadside tourist attraction. Greer was a controversial figure, said to always be looking for a way to turn a buck. The stories go that he lured tourists to stop by offering to fill their jugs with free cold, pure mountain water. That gave him an opportunity to convince them to tour the historic battlefield—for a small fee, of course. Greer also claimed that the well on Pigeon's Ranch was the oldest in the United States. This claim was unfounded, but it made for good publicity. Bears were also part of this historic roadside attraction's allure; one particularly ornery black bear constantly harassed tourists and gave Greer trouble.

The bears were gone by the mid-1940s, and in 1966 Glorieta Pass Battlefield, upon which Pigeon's Ranch sits, was listed on the National Register of Historic Places. Today, the one remaining historically significant building on Pigeon's Ranch sits precariously close to NM 50—one wayward vehicle and the irreplaceable structure would be, shall we say, history. NM 50 also slices through the Glorieta Battlefield, making public access to the Civil War site difficult and dangerous. Strong efforts are being made to reroute NM 50 around the battlefield and to restore the area to its Santa Fe Trail and Civil War–era appearance.

LA BAJADA HILL, LA BAJADA
c. 1926

The origins of this infamous hill go back more than 400 years, when it was known as the *Camino Real de Tierra Adentro* and used as a footpath and wagon trail. The U.S. military began to regularly use La Bajada Hill ("the descent" in Spanish) after the Civil War. Soon the wagon road became the main route from Santa Fe to Albuquerque and was used by all types of traffic, including commercial stagecoach lines.

By 1910 adventurous automobile drivers were navigating the old wagon ruts, and in the early 1910s the state highway engineer ordered improvements to the road. Rock retaining walls and a new gravel surface improved the road somewhat. In the 1920s the road, by then known as National Old Trails Highway, was rerouted at the top end of the climb to make travel safer. On November 11, 1926, this portion of the road officially became U.S. Highway 66. From 1926 to 1932 the mere mention of La Bajada Hill struck terror in the hearts and minds of Route 66 motorists. The descent snaked 1.4 miles down the hill at a 6 percent grade and an elevation drop of over 500 feet. This, coupled with hazardous switchbacks, rattled the composure of many motorists. Ascending the hill, you had other worries. In the early days of the automobile fuel tanks were mounted above the carburetors. The ascent was so steep that many automobiles had to travel up the hill in reverse to allow fuel to feed the carburetor.

In 1932 Highway 66 was routed 3 miles east to the same route currently used by Interstate 25. Today, after 50-plus years of erosion and neglect, La Bajada is only traversable with high-clearance four-wheel-drive vehicles.

THE BIG CUT, DOMINGO
c. 1926

Sitting north of Algodones and south of Domingo on the San Felipe Indian Reservation, the Big Cut was part of the El Camino Real Highway, built in 1905 by the New Mexico Territorial Road Commission. A 60-foot cut was carved through the foothills of the Sandia Mountain with nothing but dynamite and men wielding picks and shovels. This pass was considered a great engineering feat for its day and second only to the roadbed built over La Bajada Hill (see page 267). On November 11, 1926, this portion of the El Camino Real Highway became U.S. Highway 66.

The cut was very narrow and allowed traffic to travel only one way, creating daily road hazards. Never paved, this section that linked Santa Rosa to Albuquerque via Santa Fe was rerouted in favor of a straight shot from Santa Rosa to Albuquerque in 1937. Part of Highway 66 for less than five full years, the "Santa Fe Loop," as it is now known, was one of the most hazardous and dangerous sections motorists faced on all of Highway 66. Lack of maintenance for over 70 years has left the Cut a victim of the elements. Once more than 60 feet deep, the Big Cut has been reduced to about 35 feet as eroding dirt and rock slowly smother the old roadbed. It is only a matter of time before this turn-of-the-century marvel is completely obliterated by the elements. All too soon, the Big Cut will fade back into the desert from whence it came and, sadly, future generations will never know what the big deal was.

RIO PUERCO
TRADING POST, RIO PUERCO
c. 1940

The Rio Puerco Trading Post was first built in the early 1940s by George Thomas Hill Jr. and his wife, Morene, 19 miles west of Albuquerque, on the south side of the post-1937 realignment of Highway 66. A fire destroyed the original trading post, and the process of rebuilding began in 1946. The updated trading post burned in the 1960s and was replaced by a new enterprise owned by the Bowlin Corporation, the same company that owns the Flying C Ranch site and many other roadside facilities in the Southwest.

Every trading post needed a gimmick, and the Rio Puerco was no exception. A full-sized stuffed polar bear standing in a glass case greeted visitors as they entered the building. One night someone broke into the trading post, broke the glass case, and made off with the bear. It was later found ripped to shreds in the Sandi Mountains outside of Albuquerque.

The Rio Puerco is home to a historically significant bridge that was preserved by the New Mexico State Highway Department. The Parker Bridge, a through truss that spanned 250 feet over the often-treacherous Rio Puerco, was fabricated by the Kansas City Structural Steel Company and completed in 1933. The bridge helped to further the cause for the much-sought-after 1937 realignment of Highway 66 that bypassed Isleta and Los Lunas. The bridge no longer handles vehicle traffic, but can be crossed and explored on foot.

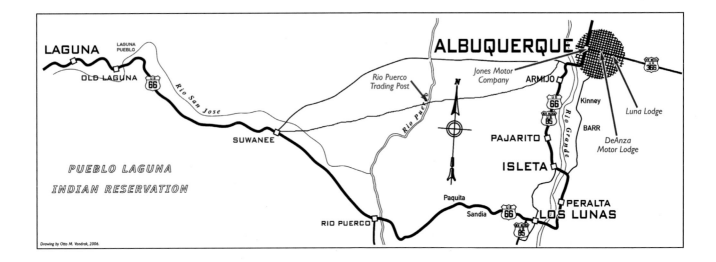

Drawing by Otto M. Vondrak, 2006.

GRANTS
c. 1950s

Grants is named for three brothers, Angus, Lewis, and John Grant, who during the late 1880s were contracted by the Atlantic & Pacific to build the railroad through the western region of New Mexico. The area first became known as Grant's Camp and when the rail line was completed and a station built, the name was changed to Grant's Station. Eventually the area became simply known as Grants.

The town of Grants grew as a farming community through the 1930s and 1940s and was most noted for its carrot fields that extended as far as 12 miles west of the town. In 1950, a Navajo rancher named Paddy Martinez discovered a "funny-looking" yellow rock in the nearby Haystack Mountains. The discovery unearthed one of largest uranium deposits in the world and changed the whole economic structure of the region. The U.S. Atomic Energy Commission contracted multiple mining companies and then bought all the uranium they could get their hands on. Grants and its surrounding area became one of the largest suppliers of uranium in the world. The mining and resulting prosperity came to a halt during the recession of 1982–1983 when the mines were forced to close up shop.

Unlike many towns along Highway 66 that suffered through the interstate bypass, the citizens of Grants managed to get through the hard times and even prosper. The town continues to grow and has become a popular tourist destination for boaters and fishermen bound for nearby Bluewater and Ramah lakes. Travel down the main street of Grants and you can still see and enjoy many Route 66–era businesses that continue to thrive despite the rush of the nearby super-slab.

JOHNNIES CAFÉ, THOREAU
C. LATE 1920s

At the time of its construction, both Johnnies and Highway 66, then a primitive dirt path, were located on the north side of the tracks in Thoreau (pronounced *thuh-roo*). In February 1936, founders Johnnie and Helen Maich sold the business to John and Anna Radosevich. John was the cook and his wife Anna did a little bit of everything, including waiting tables. The small café was only 20x40 and consisted of a counter with a couple of stools and four tables. In its early years, the food was prepared on a Coleman wood stove and dishes were washed with water heated by a wood fire. A one-cylinder diesel generator was pressed into service to supply electricity for

lights during the evening hours. Shortly after John and Anna purchased the café, Route 66 was rerouted to the south side of the tracks. Johnnies itself was moved, building and all, to its current location along side the new alignment in 1947. In 1949 an addition was made to the building's east side, and in the early 1950s another section was built on to the west side. Today, the western addition is an off-sale liquor store. Johnnies was well known in the area for serving outstanding chili and thick steaks. "People would drive from Gallup just for the chili," says John Radosevich, whose family still owns the building.

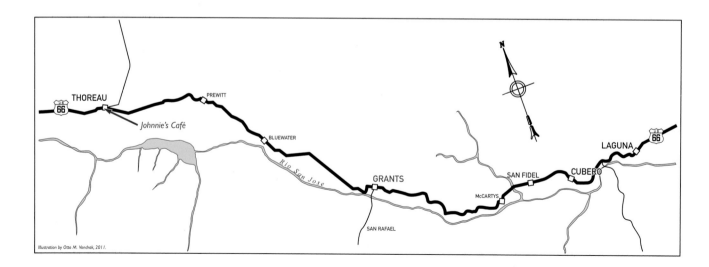

Illustration by Otto M. Vondrak, 2011.

JOHNNIES CAFE, THOREAU, N. MEX.

GOOD EATS

Reasonable Prices   Tourist Headquarters

U. S. HIGHWAY 66

Mileage from Johnnies Cafe

WEST TO		EAST TO	
Continental Divide	5	Grants	31
Gallup, N. Mexico	32	Laguna	65
Painted Desert	106	Los Lunas	116
Petrified Forest	118	Albuquerque	139
Holbrook, Ariz.	134	Domingo	176
Winslow	167	Santa Fe	203
Flagstaff	230	Las Vegas	277
Maine	250	Trinidad, Colo.	418
Grand Canyon	315	**NORTH TO**	
Williams	266	Crown Point	28
Needles, Cal.	470	Chaco Canyon	60
Los Angeles	770	**SOUTH TO**	
		Albuquerque	139
		El Paso	444

NAVAJO LODGE, COOLIDGE
c. 1936

Living through the bitter cold Canadian winters did not sit well with Merle and Daisy Muncy, so in 1936, they packed everything up and moved south to New Mexico. The Muncys settled on a plot 20 miles east of Gallup in a town named for President Calvin Coolidge. (Prior to 1926 the town had been variously named Bacon Springs, Cranes Station, Coolidge—for the director of the Atlantic & Pacific Railroad—Dewey, Crane, and Guam.) There the Muncys proceeded to build the Navajo Lodge, replicating a Spanish hacienda. The business included a store, motel, service station, and a bar and restaurant.

Chicken dinners at the Navajo Lodge were legendary and a favorite among tourists and locals, but it was Saturday nights that the Navajo Lodge really started hopping. Folks from as far as Gallup to the east and Bluewater to the west and beyond would come to cut loose at the weekly Saturday night dances.

When World War II rolled around, the economic climate took a turn for the worse and business at the Navajo Lodge followed suit.

After taking jobs at nearby Fort Wingate during the war, the Muncys sold the business to another couple, Alexander and Melvina Lavasek from Chicago.

During the late 1940s roadside businesses began sprouting up along Route 66 in increasing numbers. Every roadside stop during this era needed some sort of gimmick to set it apart and attract customers. To accomplish this, the Lavaseks drafted a couple of bears into service. Tillie and Millie were chained to a tree and trained to drink the soda from bottles given to them by customers. Sometime in the 1960s, the Lavaseks retired and the soda-drinking bears were shipped off to a zoo somewhere in New Mexico.

The Navajo Lodge is owned and operated today by Sherwood and Roberta Stauder. No longer the roadside tourist stop of yesteryear, the lodge is lovingly maintained as a bed and breakfast. The grounds and surrounding area are breathtaking and definitely worth an overnight stay or at the very least a visit.

P-489 NAVAJO LODGE -COOLIDGE, N.M., 21 MILES EAST OF GALLUP ON U.S. HIGHWAY 66. S.W. Post Card Co. Albuquerque

GALLUP
c. 1958

David L. Gallup established an office and pay station for the Atlantic & Pacific Railroad here in 1880. When the tracks through the area were finally completed in 1881, the town officially became known as Gallup. The railroad selected Gallup as a division terminal in 1895 and for the next 40 years coalmining and railroading dominated the economy. Trading with the Zuni, Navajo, and Hopi tribes, well-known for their fine arts and crafts, also played an important role in Gallup's economy, and does to this day.

The late 1940s through the 1950s and into the 1960s saw tremendous growth in Gallup as its city limits expanded in all directions. The Mother Road was the artery feeding this expansion, as legions of motorists flocked to the West. Motels with names such as the Blue Spruce Lodge, Arrowhead Lodge, Zia Motel, and Thunderbird Motel popped up all through town, creating a brightly lit neon jungle. Although not as hectic as it once was, Gallup continues to be a major stopover for motorists traveling in either direction.

Many buildings listed on the National Register of Historic Places survive along Route 66 and Coal Avenue (original 66) through town, including the El Rancho Hotel and the El Morro Theater. In addition, 6 miles east of Gallup, the Red Rock State Park hosts the annual Inter-Tribal Indian Ceremonial. The largest gathering of Native American tribes in the country attracts tourists from around the world.

Arrowhead Lodge Motel   Gallup, New Mexico
In the Heart of the Indian Country — East Side on U. S. Highway 66

ARROWHEAD LODGE, GALLUP
c. 1948

Gallup's overnight lodging facilities were developed in two distinct areas and built in somewhat different eras. The west-side motel row was developed from the early 1950s through the 1960s and beyond. Motels on this side of town were only built on the south side of Route 66 since the proximity of the Santa Fe Railway yard and tracks left no room for development. The east side began development in 1946 when the railroad made available a limited number of construction sites within the city limits. These sites, located on a narrow strip of land between Route 66 and the tracks, attracted dozens of investors hoping to cash in on the burgeoning post–World War II tourist trade. The proximity of the land to the ever popular El Rancho Hotel made investing in the motel business even more attractive to potential owners. Soon the Gallup night sky was awash with the soft glow of neon. These cleverly designed signs were designed with one thing in mind: to grab your attention—especially away from the throngs of nearby competition.

The Arrowhead Lodge was one of these newly built motels advertised as "ultra modern." Built in the late 1940s, the Arrowhead Lodge, still in operation today, sits on that narrow strip of land made available by the Santa Fe. The 25-unit motel was designed in a U shape with a small landscaped courtyard in the center. The courtyard was eventually home to a playground for children. The motel office is located on the front of the building's east side, just steps away from Route 66. For some unknown reason, in the 1960s the beautiful original arrowhead-shaped neon sign was replaced with a more modern-looking version. Boasting Serta mattresses, Panel Ray heat, and air conditioning, the Arrowhead Lodge became a popular overnight stay for tourists and businessmen alike. And with its close proximity to the El Rancho, tourists on a budget could stay at the Arrowhead and still take advantage of the El Rancho's fine restaurant and bar facilities. This no doubt was a plus for the Arrowhead's popularity.

EL RANCHO HOTEL, GALLUP
c. 1937

As you enter the historic El Rancho through the stately front entry, you immediately realize this was and still is a special place. The El Rancho was built by Hollywood director "Griff" Griffith, brother of Hollywood mogul D. W. Griffith, and officially opened on December 17, 1937. Griff arrived in Gallup to shoot a movie in the early 1930s, quickly fell in love with the area, and later returned to open the hotel. From the 1940s through to the 1960s, the region surrounding Gallup developed into a popular film location and became the backdrop for dozens of Hollywood productions. During its heyday, the El Rancho Hotel was one of the premier hotels in the entire Southwest and became *the* place for the Hollywood set to stay when filming in the area. Stars who stayed there included Kirk Douglas, Spencer Tracy, Katherine Hepburn, and future President Ronald Reagan. Autographed photos of these stars and many others grace the walls of a second-story balcony that overlooks the magnificent main lobby. To reach this mezzanine, one climbs either of two curving staircases on each side of a gigantic stone fireplace. The polished-brick lobby floor was always maintained to a high gloss. Navajo rugs hung on the walls completed the lobby's classic rustic western ambience.

During its glory years the El Rancho was the definition of luxury and included many amenities that were lacking in other typical tourist hotels of the day, including a beauty parlor, barbershop, and full maid service. A fine dining room, coffee shop, and bar were also provided for guest convenience. During its later years, the hotel traded hands several times. This lack of steady ownership, as well as the interstate bypass, contributed to the El Rancho's slow decline and eventually led to its closing in 1987. The final indignant blow occurred when the hotel's fine furniture and unique furnishings were unceremoniously dragged out to the parking lot and auctioned off.

Armond Ortega, who as a boy admired the hotel, bought the El Rancho in 1988. With much effort he worked at tracing and acquiring the original furnishings. Although many of the hotel's unique pieces were unattainable, he successfully re-created the classic ambience of the old hotel. The El Rancho was listed on the National Register of Historic Places on January 14, 1988.

For 50 years, the El Rancho Hotel greeted guests along Route 66 with class and dignity. Outside its front doors, the hotel was witness to the growth of Highway 66 from a narrow two-lane road to a wider two-lane highway and eventually to a four-lane road and the Interstate 40 bypass. Luckily for us, this one-of-a-kind hotel once again greets guests with open arms and enjoys the renewed worldwide interest in Route 66 and its landmarks.

LOG CABIN LODGE, GALLUP
c. 1952

Tony and Francis Leone built the Log Cabin Lodge in 1937. Originally, it consisted of six log cabins and a single-story office building. A fireplace in each cabin provided ambience and heat during the cold winter nights. "Every day, each cabin was set up with a supply of paper and logs for an evening fire" says Lois Berger, daughter of Tony and Francis. Each cabin also featured a kitchenette, all of which were eventually eliminated because of the added time required to clean up after guests. Beds replaced the kitchen appliances, adding extra sleeping space to each cabin. Navajo rugs and taxidermy filled the roomy lobby that also offered a large central fireplace.

During the 1940s and 1950s the Log Cabin Lodge was part of the Best Western chain and two double log cabins were added, as well as a whole new wing built in an adobe style with side-by-side rooms and attached garages. The property was sold around 1959, but the new owner was unable to keep up with the mortgage payments and the lodge reverted back to the Leones. Multiple owners followed, but time took its toll on the landmark. Maintenance and upkeep over the years were sorely lacking and the Log Cabin Lodge eventually fell into a dismal state of disrepair.

The Log Cabin Lodge was listed on the National Register of Historic Places in 1993, but that was not enough to forestall the inevitable. The lodge served its last guest in the mid-1990s and subsequently began its slide into a terminal state of disrepair, becoming home to transients, drug dealers, and worse. The estimated cost for restoration was in the millions and well beyond what most investors considered viable. Deemed an eyesore by most citizens of Gallup, it was ordered condemned without hesitation. On May 14, 2004, one of the most distinctive overnight stays along the entire route was razed.

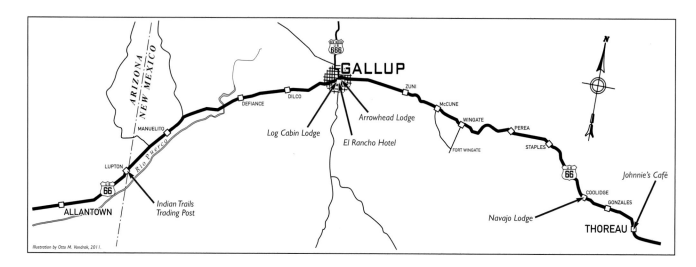

Illustration by Otto M. Vondrak, 2011.

LOG CABIN LODGE
GALLUP, NEW MEXICO

U. S. Highway 66, ¼ Mile West of Business Center

When U.S. Highway 66 was designated in 1926, existing roads, variations of Beale Wagon Road and other old trails, were stitched together from town to town to form the fledgling highway. Highway 66 entered Arizona from the east via Lupton and continued through Holbrook, Winslow, Winona, Flagstaff, Williams, Ash Fork, Seligman, Peach Springs, Kingman, Oatman, and finally Topock.

U.S. Highway 66 originally spanned 385 miles across northern Arizona, and, as in other states, a vast majority of the road was dirt and poorly maintained. As traffic grew, motels, cafés, and service stations sprang up to accommodate travelers, and each town stretched its city limits as more and more businesses vied for the tourist dollar. By 1934 most of the Mother Road in Arizona was paved. Near the end of 1937 paving was complete across Arizona, which also saw its fair share of alignment changes over the years. In 1953 the perilous hairpin path from Kingman to Oatman over Sitgreaves Pass was eliminated in favor of a straighter route bypassing Oatman via Yucca on its way to Topock. In the May 1955 issue of *Arizona Highways* it was reported that 2,999 vehicles used Route 66 in Arizona every day, or 1,094,635 vehicles per year, of which 73 percent were from out of state. In 1955, the magazine added, the total length of Route 66 through Arizona was 376 miles, with 174.8 being constructed to the minimum 40-foot width, the Interstate standard.

Construction of Interstate 40 in Arizona was full speed ahead in the 1960s, and by 1969 most rural sections of Route 66 were upgraded or replaced. The first city to be bypassed was Flagstaff in 1968, but construction of other city bypasses moved at a much slower rate and it wasn't until 1978 that the next city, Winslow, saw a bypass. That same year the Interstate opened from Seligman to Kingman, leaving numerous small towns in an economic nosedive, including Peach Springs, which holds the dubious honor of being bypassed by 36 miles, the most of any city on the route. Holbrook, Joseph City, Ash Fork, and Kingman were all bypassed in 1981, but it wasn't until October 13, 1984, that Williams became the last city on the entire route to be bypassed.

Route 66 across Arizona is a study in scenic contrasts as one travels west from the wide-open spaces of the eastern high desert on a gradual climb through the beautiful, dense pine forests east of Flagstaff to Williams. From Williams, at an elevation of 7,000 feet, 66 drops abruptly down Ash Fork Hill to just over 5,000 feet in about 6 miles. From Ash Fork, the route travels west past Seligman, where the landscape changes again and the treeless expanse of the Aubrey Valley comes into view. From there, the road gradually descends over rolling hills to Kingman at 3,328 feet, eventually reaching the low desert terrain of Topock and the Colorado River, where the elevation is a mere 507 feet above sea level. Much of the Mother Road in Arizona lies directly beneath the path of Interstate 40. Nevertheless, there are still many sections of the old road that survive and are well worth the time to explore them.

INDIAN TRAILS
TRADING POST, LUPTON
c. 1947

During the heyday of Highway 66, service stations, curio shops, and trading posts dotted the western stretch of "America's Main Street." Among the most colorful were four establishments located along the state line between New Mexico and Arizona: the State Line Trading Post, Fort Chief Yellowhorse, the Box Canyon Trading Post, and, perhaps the most popular, the Indian Trails Trading Post.

Max and Amelia Ortega established the Indian Trails Trading Post in 1946. In the beginning, local Navajo business was the mainstay, but Max soon expanded the small trading post into a full-service travel stop. As the business grew, the Ortega name became synonymous with fine handcrafted Indian jewelry, and to this day son Armond continues to be one of the largest Indian jewelry dealers in the world. Armond also went on to purchase and revitalize the landmark El Rancho Hotel in nearby Gallup, New Mexico.

Today a handful of the old trading posts, including Fort Chief Yellowhorse, remain open, but only memories of the Indian Trails Trading Post remain. In 1965 Interstate 40 was completed from the New Mexico border to a few miles west of Lupton.

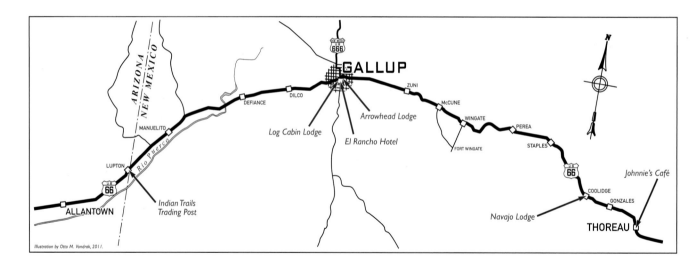

Illustration by Otto M. Vondrak, 2011.

PAINTED DESERT
TRADING POST, NAVAJO
c. 1942

Imagine the loneliest, most sun-baked desert expanse conceivable, where a single lizard might be the only living thing—other than yourself—for miles. There, right smack dab in the middle of lonely, you will find the Painted Desert Trading Post. Dotch and Alberta Windsor opened the Painted Desert Trading Post in the early 1940s, selling Indian curios, cold drinks, and sandwiches, as well as gasoline from gravity pumps. The trading post had no telephone, so calls were placed at the Painted Desert Park several miles to the west. Appliances ran on electricity generated by a windmill. The Windsors operated the post together until their marriage ended around 1950. Joy Nevin, who ran a veterinary supply business in Holbrook, Arizona,

met Dotch at the trading post during a business trip and the couple married, with Joy giving birth to a daughter in 1952. Dotch and Joy operated the trading post together until they divorced in 1956.

The section of Route 66 that ran past the business was relocated, widened, and designated Interstate 40 in the late 1950s, and the trading post has sat empty and abandoned ever since. Joy went on to become a leading figure in nearby Holbrook, where a street is named in her honor. Dotch died in October 1964, but the skeletal remains of the Painted Desert Trading Post still sit alongside the abandoned roadway, slowly being reclaimed by the desert that once gave it life.

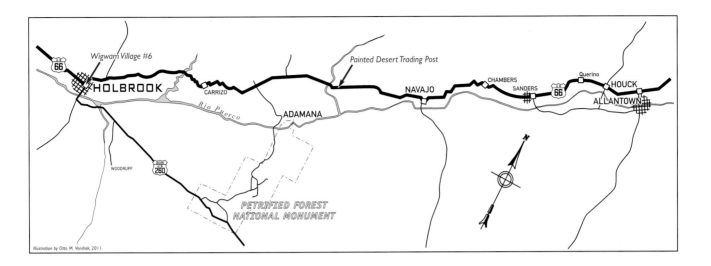

Illustration by Otto M. Vondrak, 2011.

HOLBROOK
c. 1935

In 1881, the Atlantic & Pacific Railroad began construction in northeast Arizona, laying track through an area known as Horsehead Crossing. A railroad station followed the next year along with a name change to Holbrook in honor of H. R. Holbrook, the railroad's first chief engineer. A post office was established on September 18, 1882, with James A. Wilson taking on the duties as first postmaster.

An important shipping depot for cattle in northeast Arizona, Holbrook was a rough-and-tumble cowboy town known as the "town too tough for women and churches." The commercial district from the 1880s through the late 1920s comprised a row of buildings on the south side of the tracks that included Wattron Drug Store and the A&B Schuster Store. The infamous Bucket of Blood Saloon was also located along this row of buildings, its name stemming from the nightly shootings and brawling that stained the wood floors. Sheriff Commodore Perry Owens is credited with bringing law and order to Holbrook, and by the end of the 1890s, the violence was all but over.

By 1929, the commercial district had moved to the north side of the tracks alongside the new Highway 66. The corner of West Hopi Drive and Navajo Boulevard became the commercial center of town. By the 1950s, West Hopi Drive was lined with motels, cafés, and service stations all cashing in on the constant flow of traffic heading out West. Holbrook enjoyed the benefit of being one of the last towns on Route 66 to be bypassed. By 1981, though, most of Arizona's Route 66 towns, including Holbrook, suffered from the interstate bypass.

The town has struggled economically ever since, with many businesses, including the motels and service stations along West Hopi Drive, shutting down. One notable exception is the Wigwam Village Motel at 811 West Hopi Drive.

WIGWAM VILLAGE #6, HOLBROOK
c. 1950

The Wigwam Village in Holbrook is arguably the most recognizable landmark on all of Route 66. It is one of seven such "villages" built in various locations across the United States from original plans developed by Frank Redford. After visiting Village #2 in Cave City, Kentucky, Chester E. Lewis returned home to Holbrook and set out to build his own Wigwam Village. Lewis purchased the rights to Redford's design and negotiated a royalty agreement for use of the Wigwam Village name. The agreement was quite unique: coin-operated radios were set up in each wigwam, and each dime spent listening to the radio was forwarded to Redford.

In the summer of 1950, Wigwam Village #6 was opened with 15 wigwams forming a U shape. (Numbered 1 through 16, there was no wigwam 13.) Each concrete-and-steel wigwam was 32 feet tall and 14 feet wide.

The motel was a complete success and was especially popular with children. What kid wouldn't want to sleep in a wigwam? The 15 wigwams captured the imagination of the traveling public and made the village *the* place to stay in Holbrook. Perhaps sleeping in a wigwam was a small part of the Wild West that tourists could still actually be a part of, even if the wigwams were made of steel and concrete and not animal skins.

When the interstate bypassed Holbrook in the mid-1970s, business waned. This downward trend continued until around 1980 when Wigwam Village saw its final overnight guest. The Wigwam Village did not suffer alone as a majority of the motels in Holbrook met the same fate.

Chester passed away in 1986, but remaining family members decided not to let Chester's dream follow him to the grave. In 1988, each wigwam structure was completely renovated, including the original polished hickory wood furniture, and was listed on the National Register of Historic Places on May 2, 2002. The Lewis family continues to own and operate Wigwam Village, ensuring future western teepee adventures for the kid in all of us.

GERONIMO TRADING POST, JOSEPH CITY
c. 1952

During the days of the Old West, trading posts were essential to our country's growth. Native Americans exchanged furs and handmade goods for merchandise such as salt and other essentials. During the golden years of Route 66, trading posts took on a whole new role. These modern posts along Highway 66 existed for one purpose and one purpose only: to separate the tourist from his cash. Instead of salt and dry goods necessary for survival, shelves offered rubber snakes, Indian trinkets, cowboy hats, and countless curios and souvenirs.

The Geronimo Trading Post was one such modern Route 66 trading post. Doc Hatfield, a resident of nearby Joseph City, opened the post in the early 1950s and named it for the renegade Apache warrior who was captured nearby and sent to prison via train out of Holbrook. Located between Holbrook and Joseph City, the Geronimo

Trading Post has thrilled souvenir seekers for over 50 years.

Karl Kempton purchased the Geronimo in 1967, and in 1974, he built the structure that houses the trading post to this day. The rocky landscape surrounding the post looks to be right out of a Hollywood western. The scenic, picturesque background complete with colorful teepees lends a certain authenticity to the place.

Today, the Geronimo Trading Post enjoys a healthy business as it continues to draw throngs of curious Route 66 tourists from around the globe. The Geronimo boasts of having "The World's Largest Petrified Tree," weighing in at a staggering 80 tons, as well as its very own interstate off-ramp. Inside you will find everything from Route 66 items and Native American crafts to rubber tomahawks and rare rock specimens, including a variety of petrified wood.

WINSLOW
c. 1938

"Standin' on a corner in Winslow, Arizona/Such a fine sight to see." The popular Eagles song of the early 1970s immortalized the corner of Second Street and Kingsley in downtown Winslow. Second Street carried Route 66 until 1951, when the ever-increasing stream of cars made it necessary to divide the flow of traffic through town. Second Street was assigned one-way traffic eastbound, and Third Street carried westbound travelers. Unfortunately, this grizzled railroad town fell on hard times when Interstate 40 bypassed it in the late 1960s and most businesses moved out nearer to the Interstate, leaving downtown Winslow looking somewhat like a ghost town.

Signs along this portion of the route commemorate the stretch as being part of the old Beale Wagon Road; other markers point out the use of this trail by Mormon immigrants in the 1870s. Wayne L. Troutner's Store for Men was the clothier of choice for locals and lonely travelers wanting to spruce up before "standin' on a corner" and hoping to be noticed by that special gal passing by in a "flatbed Ford." Like so many roadside business owners along Route 66, Troutner was innovative when it came to roadside advertising, and created quite a stir when he placed billboards depicting a vivacious young cowgirl along Route 66 and other highways out West. The billboards became popular worldwide with sightings reported as far away as Paris and Guam.

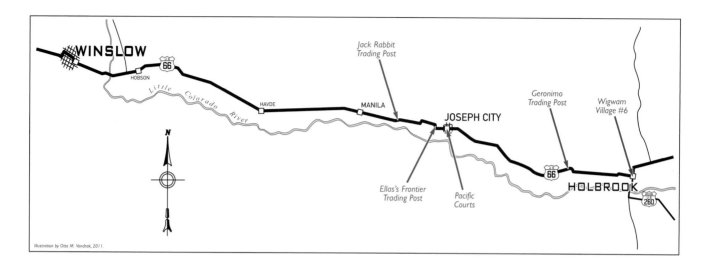

Illustration by Otto M. Vondrak, 2011.

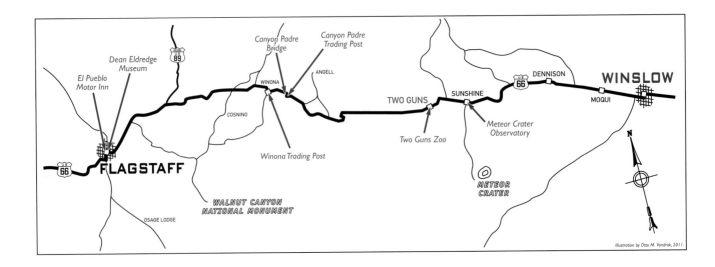

Illustration by Otto M. Vondrak, 2011.

METEOR CRATER OBSERVATORY, WEST OF WINSLOW
c. 1946

Harry and Hope Locke began work on the impressive, castle-like Meteor Crater Observatory structure in the mid-1930s. Despite Hope's passing, Harry continued work on the building, and in the late 1930s finally opened the observatory to the public. A few years later, the Meteor Crater Observatory closed its doors due to lack of visitors and the large debt accrued during its construction. Then, in 1946, Dr. Harvey H. Nininger leased the building and on October 19 opened the doors once again. Inspired by a meteor he saw while teaching in Kansas in 1923, Dr. Nininger dedicated his life to the study of hurtling space debris and is known as the founder of the scientific study of meteorites.

The crater itself was located about 6 miles south of the observatory. Visitors climbed the dark and very narrow stairs of the tower and waited their turn at the telescope—all for only 25 cents! The museum also housed concessions, meteorite samples, and a detailed model showing the path Arizona's meteor took as it sailed through the earth's atmosphere, eventually crashing to the desert floor. A few years after its reopening the facility became officially known as the American Meteorite Museum. Visible for many miles, it must have been a remarkable site. Even today the ruins can be seen out in the distance on Interstate 40, beckoning to passing cars. The Meteorite Museum hosted its last stargazer in 1953. Dr. Nininger died in 1986.

TWO GUNS
c. 1948

Located halfway between Winslow and Flagstaff, no other town on Route 66 has such a frightening and storied past. In 1881, the story goes, more than 50 Navajo men, women, and children were slaughtered by a band of Apaches at a Navajo camp in the nearby Painted Desert. Navajo warriors tracked the Apaches, trapped them in a nearby cave, and quickly gathered sagebrush, wood, and anything else that would burn. The Navajos then built a fire at the entrance to the cave, which quickly filled with fire and smoke, then opened fire into the cave. They entered it the next day to find the charred and riddled remains of 42 Apaches. The cave is still known as the Apache Death Cave and carries with it a curse of bad luck to anyone who enters or disturbs the site. Other legends include rumors of loot left in a nearby canyon by train robbers.

By the 1950s, Two Guns had become a very popular stop along Route 66. What kid wouldn't want to see the Indian cliff dwellings, mountain lions, and the occasional cowboy or Indian? Stores, cafés, a service station, and a motel were also there for tired tourists. The concrete bridge through town crosses the Canyon Diablo and was listed on the National Register of Historic Places in 1988. The former roadside stop is now a crumbling ghost town. Stop and visit at your own risk.

WINONA TRADING POST, WINONA
c. 1955

In the early 1920s Billy Adams built a one-story rock structure from river stones and nearby Indian ruins and called it the Winona Trading Post. He offered necessities for modern motorists, including fan belts, coils, tools, and tires. Cold drinks and dry goods were also available. In 1924 a post office was established in the trading post, and Myrtle Adams became the first female postmaster in Arizona. Soon after completing the trading post, Billy Adams and his sons built 10 small wooden cabins, said to comprise one of the first motor courts in the United States. Each cabin measured 10x14 feet and featured a wood-burning stove, mirror, and washstand. In 1925, Adams built the two-story Winona Motel, once again of stone. The motel had 14 rooms upstairs and a small lobby below. Through the 1940s it was a beehive of activity, especially during World War II when convoys of troops would come through town. Billy's son Ralph recalls, "They would buy every bottle of pop and every candy bar we had and run us out completely in one visit."

The early 1950s saw a realignment of Route 66 to its current location, and a new trading post, including a cafe, tourist cabins, and service station, was built alongside the new alignment. Billy Adams and his family eventually left the post to become ranchers. The current owners bulldozed the motel, trading post, and campground.

DEAN ELDREDGE MUSEUM, FLAGSTAFF
c. 1931

The day young Dean Eldredge found a petrified frog in his childhood state of Wisconsin, he was committed to a lifetime of collecting and preserving rare artifacts, curios, and oddities. His passion for collecting and preserving eventually led him to an interest in taxidermy, and in 1918, he began his career as a professional taxidermist.

Eldredge was a well-known adventurer and spent a good portion of the 1920s on collecting trips throughout the United States and Mexico. In 1930, he bought a piece of land on the outskirts of Flagstaff with the notion of building a showcase for his eclectic collection, which included six-legged sheep, two-headed calves, and traditional western and Indian artifacts. This property was more than 3 miles from the downtown business district and was considered very rural at the time, but Eldredge felt that the location would be the perfect spot for his museum because westbound tourists would easily spot it among the first businesses on their approach to Flagstaff. Soon after purchasing the land, he hired out-of-work lumberjacks to cut trees and haul logs to his newly purchased property where he built what he once touted as the "biggest log cabin in the world." That claim was a bit far fetched, and he soon revised it to the "biggest log cabin in Arizona."

The Dean Eldredge Museum opened for business on June 20, 1931. Packed with over 30,000 items, the museum hosted thousands of fascinated tourists who gawked at his incredible collection of oddities and unusual artifacts. Navajo rugs were hung from ceiling beams and walls and covered floors. Every possible square inch of the place was utilized for museum pieces as well as gift items. Hopi pottery, Indian baskets, and Navajo rugs were among the fine Native American crafts sold at the museum. Examples of taxidermy were everywhere, and locals soon nicknamed the museum "The Zoo." The name stuck, and 75 years later locals still it so. Sadly, the museum and trading post operated for only five years when its owner succumbed to cancer. After his death, Eldredge's collection, which took a lifetime to amass, was regrettably sold off. The museum building was purchased by Doc Williams who opened a nightclub there in 1936. Cashing in on the end of Prohibition, the establishment was extremely successful.

Over the subsequent years, the building underwent several changes that included a recording studio and eventually a shady beer-drinking, fist-throwing roadhouse. Don Scott, a successful musician with the likes of Bob Wills' Texas Playboys, along with his wife Thorna, purchased the property in 1963. They cleaned the place up and turned it into a popular country music concert and dance hall featuring western swing music. With a little help from friends such as Willie Nelson and Waylon Jennings, the Museum Club quickly became a hot country-western showcase and a favorite stop for many big-time and aspiring country stars on their way to Las Vegas.

Don and Thorna managed and operated the club for 10 years while living in an upstairs apartment until tragedy struck in 1973. One evening after closing the club, Thorna slipped and fell down the stairs that led to their apartment. She suffered a broken neck and fell into a coma, dying a few weeks later. Constantly surrounded by reminders of that deadly evening, Don took his own life in 1975. Many believe that Don and Thorna Scott have never left the club and continue to inhabit the building. Their ghosts are said to haunt the Museum Club, startling guests and employees on a regular basis. Lights turning off and on, displaced bar items, and sporadic appearances of a ghostly female figure climbing the back stairway have all been reported. Many employees have also been perplexed by strange sightings of Thorna sitting in a dimly lit booth while unwitting patrons offer to buy her a drink.

Despite the footsteps and creaking floors, Martin and Stacie Zanzucchi bought the club in 1978 with a mind to renovate and restore some of the old "feel" of the original Dean Eldredge Museum. Stuffed animals were hung on walls and vintage furnishings were carefully purchased. Today, vintage Route 66 memorabilia also abounds. The Museum Club firmly captures the feel of a bygone era when music rang out from under the doors and through open windows of roadhouses in every town from Chicago to Los Angeles. Martin and Stacie continue to operate the Museum Club and offer the finest in country-western music and dancing. Martin is also a director of the Route 66 Association in Arizona and the man responsible for the renaming Santa Fe Avenue through Flagstaff to Route 66. While in Flagstaff, stop in and say hello, listen to some fine country music, do a little dancing, and maybe even see a ghost or two. Hey, who ordered this drink?

EL PUEBLO MOTOR INN, FLAGSTAFF
c. 1940

E. B. Goble, a local contractor, built the El Pueblo Motor Inn for Philip Johnston in 1936. Born in 1892, Johnston was the son of a Navajo missionary and is best known as the man responsible for developing the Navajo "Code Talkers" program during World War II. Growing up on the reservation as a child, he learned to speak fluent Navajo, and the complex code he developed based on this unwritten language stumped the Japanese throughout the war and saved countless American lives.

The El Pueblo Motor Inn is located 3 miles east of downtown Flagstaff "in the heart of the Old West," as proclaimed on the back of an advertising postcard. The area was considered "out in the country" when the motel was built. The El Pueblo was quite successful in its day, due in no small part to the fact that it was one of the first auto courts travelers came across when approaching the city from the east. The rooms were set back from the road in a beautiful wooded area dense with pine trees. It didn't hurt that picturesque mountains formed the backdrop. "Modern comfort in the pines" and "your home away from home" were a couple of the advertising catch phrases Johnston used to attract passing motorists.

Johnston died in 1978, but his El Pueblo Motor Inn still stands among the pines today. Granted, time, the elements, and a string of neglectful owners have taken a toll on the landmark motel. A couple of the rooms continue to be rented on a nightly basis, but most units are currently utilized as monthly rental apartments. Nevertheless, the El Pueblo Motor Inn remains a prime example of the classic 1930s-era motor court.

FLAGSTAFF
c. 1950

Settlers began arriving in what is now the Flagstaff area around 1876, and sheepherder Thomas Forsythe MacMillan is commonly credited as the area's first permanent resident. Legend has it that on July 4, 1876, settlers stripped a giant Ponderosa pine and raised an American flag in honor of the nation's centennial. Subsequently, they named the area "Flag Staff," and upon the opening of the post office in 1881 the town became known as Flagstaff. A year later the Atlantic & Pacific Railroad rolled into town, securing the town's future.

Fire destroyed the settlement in 1886 and 1888, but it was quickly rebuilt in both instances. In 1894 Dr. Percival Lowell was attracted to Flagstaff by its clear skies and established the world-famous Lowell Observatory, where in 1930 the planet Pluto was discovered.

Flagstaff sits on the Colorado Plateau at the foot of the San Francisco Peaks and has the honor of being the highest point on all of Route 66. Highway 66 through town is home to many historic structures, including the Museum Club, a well-known roadhouse built in 1931. Listed on the National Register of Historic Places in 1994, the Museum Club continues to attract tourists with its vintage atmosphere.

West on Route 66 past the Museum Club is Flagstaff's "Motel Row." Many fine examples of 1930s and 1940s motels line this strip, albeit in varying states of repair. In 1968 Interstate 40 replaced Route 66 through Flagstaff, making it the first city in Arizona to be bypassed. In fact, it would be a full decade before another Arizona Route 66 town was bypassed.

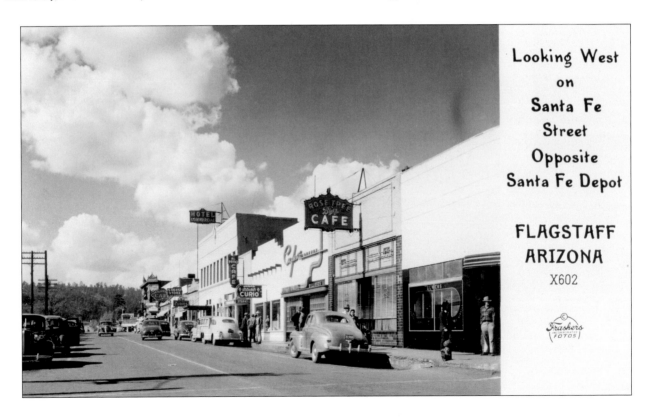

Looking West on Santa Fe Street Opposite Santa Fe Depot

FLAGSTAFF ARIZONA

X602

PARKS IN THE PINES
GENERAL STORE, PARKS
c. 1929

The town of Parks was originally known as Rhodes, but its name was changed to Maine in 1898 in honor of the famous battleship sunk in Havana Harbor that year. Realizing there was another town in the territory called Maine, the U.S. Postal Service forced the town to find a new name. As it happened, a man by the name of Parks operated a general store and early post office in town, and it was agreed to change the name of the town to Parks in honor of this pioneer shopkeeper.

The original town site was located 2 miles east of its present location, but was moved when the first highway came through. By 1921 the Old Trails Highway was completed and quickly became well traveled as the numbers of automobile tourists grew. Soon there was a need for a good road to the Grand Canyon. Flagstaff and Williams fought over the right to have the new road begin in their town. It was deemed fair to split the difference, and the road was built from Parks. This new road was completed in June 1921.

In November of that same year, Art Anderson and Don McMillan, filling a growing need to serve these masses of tourists, built a general store and gas station at the intersection of the Old Trails Highway and the new road to the Grand Canyon. The original historic building still stands and houses a store and post office. The Flagstaff Chamber of Commerce built the stone columns and sign over the road around the same time as the opening of the store in 1921.

In 1926 the Old Trails Highway was designated Highway 66. In 1928 flamboyant promoter C. C. Pyle (also known as "Cash and Carry" Pyle) organized a footrace to promote the new highway. Billed as "C. C. Pyle's 1st Annual International Trans-Continental Footrace," the contest became more affectionately known as the Bunion Derby. The race began March 4 at Ascot Speedway in Los Angeles and followed Highway 66 to Chicago before continuing to Madison Square Garden in New York City. The athletes ran an average of 40 miles a day through municipalities Pyle could convince to pay a fee. Andy Payne, a farm boy from Oklahoma, won, reaching New York on March 26 and claiming the $25,000 prize. Payne (No. 43) is shown at right passing the Parks in the Pines General Store.

Very little has changed about the building since the store's opening in 1921. The old wood floor strains and creaks with every step, the vintage furnishings hide tales of bygone eras, and the post office inside recalls an earlier time. In 2000 Ron and Millie Gillpatrick purchased the Parks store and continue its fine tradition of serving delicious homemade sandwiches to locals and travelers alike.

WILLIAMS
c. 1940s

Founded in 1876, Williams was named for the famed mountaineer William Sherley Williams. The railroad officially arrived in town in 1882, and Williams quickly grew into a lumber and ranching center. In 1901, the Santa Fe Railway built a 60-mile spur to the Grand Canyon, and Williams has since been known as the "Gateway to the Grand Canyon." By the turn of the century, Williams, like many western railroad towns, had a rough-and-tumble reputation, its streets lined with brothels, saloons, opium dens, and gambling houses. One would be hard pressed to find any evidence of that reputation today. This quaint, small town has changed little since Route 66 carried the masses west and grape Nehi was the drink of the day. One can walk the streets, lined with many fine motels and cafés, and feel magically transported to a different time, when life's hectic pace was a crawl compared to today. All this thanks largely to the fact that Williams (nicknamed "Little Las Vegas" in late 1930s for its abundant neon signage) holds the honor of being the last bypassed town on Route 66; the final 6 miles of Interstate 40 bypassed the town on October 13, 1984. That same year, the Downtown Business District of Williams was placed on the National Register of Historic Places. The population, holding at about 3,000, has not changed much in 60 years—no doubt the residents like it that way.

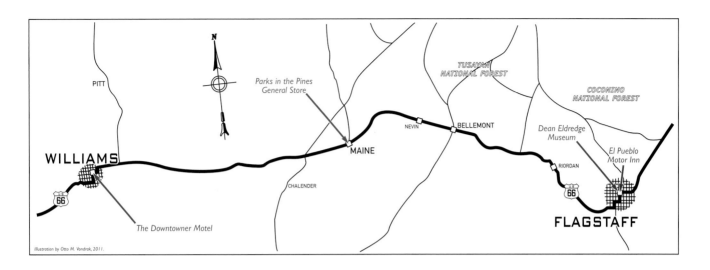

Illustration by Otto M. Vondrak, 2011.

THE DOWNTOWNER MOTEL, WILLIAMS
c. 1952

Built during the tourist explosion of the early 1950s, the Downtowner Motel remains a fine example of the modern-styled tourist motels of the era and utilizes the classic U-shaped design. Unfortunately for the owners, the U shape of the motel was doomed from the start. With the massive increase in automobile travel, Williams was overloaded with traffic. Sometime in the mid-1950s, engineers decided to split east and west traffic through town into two one-way streets. Bill Williams Avenue would carry eastbound traffic, while Railroad Avenue would carry westbound travelers.

This split created a logistics problem for the motel and its owner: access to the Downtowner from the west was essentially eliminated. To solve the problem, a portion of the rear of the motel was removed. In its place a driveway was built to allow motel access for westbound traffic.

A part of the Best Western chain and an American Automobile Association recommended motel, the Downtowner was a popular stopover. In 1988, Sam Vaidya purchased the motel and initiated some much-needed maintenance. Vaidya vows to preserve the classic look and feel of his 18-unit motel. He understands the importance of Williams and its relationship to Highway 66. Williams has the distinction of being the last town along the entire route to be bypassed, a somber event that took place on October 13, 1984. That same year the Downtown District of Williams became a National Register Historic District, and in 1989 Route 66 through Williams was listed on the National Register of Historic Places.

THE DOWNTOWNER MOTEL, WILLIAMS, ARIZONA

COPPER STATE COURT, ASH FORK
c. 1939

Copper State Court began as a Standard Oil station and general store in 1924, two years before the main street through Ash Fork became Highway 66. Situated on the east side of the once-bustling town, the Copper State Court was the creation of Ezell and Zelma Nelson. Prior to establishing the Copper State, the Nelsons were employed at the Harvey House in Kingman, Arizona. Seeking a better life for themselves, they set out to build a business of their own. The Nelsons realized their vision in 1928 when they finished adding a 12-cottage motel to the gas station and general store. The business became known as the Copper State Modern Cottages.

The cottages are set up in the classic L shape, and the office is tucked in the western corner. Each cottage was meticulously built using white river rock held together with black mortar. The natural stone survived until it was deemed necessary to do something to attract the attention of passing motorists, and the exteriors of the units were painted a stark white. Not only was this gambit successful, but it also gave the impression of cleanliness, which of course remains a very important virtue to potential guests.

Hardwood floors were featured throughout each of the units. Eventually the hardwood was removed from the bathrooms and replaced with concrete. Other than that, all of the original hardwood remains intact. Room size varies from unit to unit but averages 12x14 feet.

Garages were situated alongside each unit, as was the norm during that era. In fact, one of the more interesting facts about this Highway 66 icon involves these garages. When the Copper State was originally built, horse travel was still a viable mode of transportation, especially in the West, and the original garages came equipped with horse railings along the inside walls. Whether used as stalls or garages, these covered spaces protected the chosen mode of transportation from the often-harsh elements. The garages have long been enclosed and now serve as storage sheds for long-term residents.

The name of the motel was eventually changed sometime during the early 1940s to the Copper State Court to keep up with the times. During the mid-1950s the gas station was remodeled to include a living space and office. Sometime during the 1960s the station closed, the gas pumps and tanks were removed, and the canopy was razed.

Both the Copper State Court and Ash Fork have had their ups and downs. During World War II, regular stops by troop trains brought thousands of service men and women through town, many of whom left a portion of their hard-earned pay in one of the local cafés or bars. The 1940s and the following years brought a deluge of vacation travelers, and the Copper State and Ash Fork hit their peak. Thousands of cars per day traveled Route 66 through town, heading west to California. Ash Fork was a beehive of activity. Sometime during the 1950s, however, the Atchison, Topeka & Santa Fe Railway moved its mainline 10 miles north of town, a move that had a profoundly negative impact on the local economy. Then, in the early 1970s, a ferocious fire destroyed many of the main-street businesses. The final insult occurred in 1979 when the interstate bypassed Ash Fork, leaving many businesses, including the Copper State Court, in the proverbial dust.

Current owners George and Brenda Bannister purchased the Copper State Court in October 1989 and have kept much of the original charm of this classic vintage motor court. The only major overhaul, according to George, was the modernization of the ancient plumbing and fixtures. He is quick to point out that the Copper State was one of the first motels in the entire region to have indoor restrooms, a feature that made the motel an extremely attractive destination for business travelers and honeymooners. He fondly remembers one morning watching a gentleman drive past the motel over a dozen times. Every time the man got close he slowed down the car but never stopped. Finally, after about a half hour or so, he stopped, got out of his car, and closely examined the grounds and the doors to every room. It turned out the man and his wife spent their honeymoon night at the Copper State Court more than 65 years earlier. "This happens on a regular basis," says George.

George is proud to report that Route 66 travelers from all over the world have stayed at the Copper State. Seven of the 12 rooms are currently rented out on a weekly or monthly basis. Room number 4 is the only unit equipped with a kitchenette and the only room that features a separate bedroom. The remaining five units are available for overnight stays.

U. S. HIGHWAY 66, EASTBOUND THROUGH ASH FORK, ARIZONA

ASH FORK
c. 1948

In 1882 the Atlantic & Pacific Railway (later merged into the Santa Fe Railway) chose for a siding stop in the area now known as Ash Fork, named for the ash trees growing at the fork of nearby Ash Creek. The Ash Fork Livestock Company drove their cattle to the railhead, then shipped the animals east by rail. The cattle business— and the town—flourished. In 1893 Ash Fork was completely decimated by a fire, but was rebuilt and relocated to the other side of the tracks, where it still stands today.

A onetime hotbed of tourist activity, Ash Fork is today a shadow of its former self. The legendary Escalante, an elegant Harvey House hotel, was built along the Santa Fe tracks in 1907 and provided rail

travelers fine dining and accommodations. In Route 66's heyday, dozens of motels, cafés, and gas stations lined the streets, offering much-needed services for travelers and vacationers. During World War II, regular troop trains brought thousands of servicepersons who eagerly spent their money there. When the Santa Fe moved its mainline 10 miles north of town in the 1950s, it marked the beginning of the end for the prosperous community. A fire destroyed many buildings in the early 1970s, and when the Interstate bypassed Ash Fork in 1979, the good times came to a screeching halt. Ash Fork, today known as the "Flagstone Capital of the U.S.A.," now sits quietly, waiting for the occasional stranded or hungry tourist.

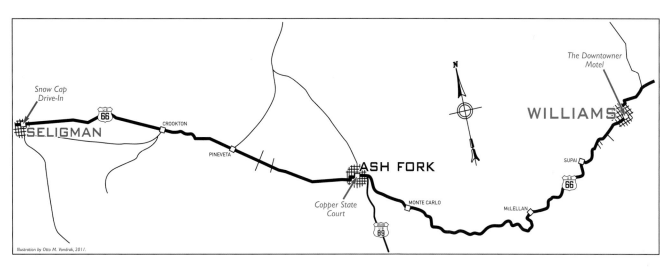

Illustration by Otto M. Vondrak, 2011.

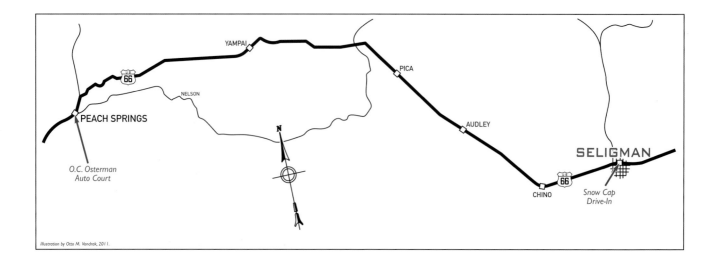

Illustration by Otto M. Vondrak, 2011.

SNOW CAP DRIVE-IN, SELIGMAN
c. 1953

Juan Delgadillo, with help from his father, built the landmark Snow Cap in 1953. A Santa Fe employee at the time, Juan used materials discarded by the railroad, earning the nickname the "Santa Fe Pack Rat." Juan at first sought to become part of the Dairy Queen network, but was turned down, so he searched for other companies to affiliate with, eventually settling on the Snow Cap Corporation of Prescott, Arizona. Snow Cap folded, but Delgadillo kept the name.

"The Snow Cap has its own life, its own humor," says son Robert Delgadillo, who works at the restaurant alongside Juan, his brother John, and sister Cecilia. Upon entering the Snow Cap, be careful not to grab the fake door handle attached to the hinged side of the door. The menu offers "Dead Chicken" and "Cheeseburgers . . . with cheese." Ask for a napkin and Juan or Robert will offer a handful of used ones. But things were not always so lighthearted. Robert says his father was a "very serious person, serious about everything." So serious that 10 years after opening the Snow Cap doctors told him he was overstressed and needed to relax or he wasn't going to be around for long. He lightened up by making his customers laugh. As he became more comfortable in that role, the high jinks became a staple. Not to give away all of Delgadillo's material, but beware of the yellow mustard bottle.

SELIGMAN
c. 1951

In the mid-1800s the area around what is today Seligman was known as Mint Valley. Settlers and pioneers traversed through the region via the Beale Wagon Road. In 1886 residents of nearby Prescott were convinced to finance a rail line called the Prescott & Arizona Central Railroad, which would connect Prescott with the Atlantic & Pacific main line via Mint Valley. With that connection, Mint Valley became known as Prescott Junction. The Prescott & Arizona Central soon went out of business, the line from Prescott Junction to Prescott was torn up, and Prescott Junction's name was changed to Seligman. It was named for two brothers who owned stock in the Atlantic & Pacific and were partners in the Aztec Land and Cattle Company.

The Atlantic & Pacific became the Atchison, Topeka & Santa Fe Railroad, or, more simply, the Santa Fe, in the late 1890s. In 1897 the Santa Fe moved its western terminus and roundhouse from Williams to Seligman, giving a huge boost to Seligman's economy. In 1905 the Santa Fe built a Harvey House dubbed El Havasu. When Highway 66 was designated in 1926, Seligman became an important stop for travelers, and once again the town reaped the benefits. Auto travel was on the rise and rail travel suffered for it. In 1954 a lack of passenger rail travel forced the Santa Fe to close the El Havasu. The building still stands and is used as office space by the BNSF Railway.

On June 29, 1956, President Dwight Eisenhower signed the Federal Highway Act, marking the beginning of the Interstate Highway System and the beginning of the end for Highway 66. On September 22, 1978, Interstate 40 bypassed Seligman. Route 66, the main street through town, suddenly fell quiet, and businesses quickly felt the effects.

Down, but not defeated, the town rallied around brothers Angel and Juan Delgadillo, who, beginning in 1985, led the current Route 66 revival and sparked new interest in the historic highway. Preaching the significance of the fabled highway to anyone who would listen, the Delgadillos were instrumental in getting the road redesignated as Historic U.S. 66. They are credited with the resurgence and increased popularity that the old road currently enjoys. Today Seligman reaps the rewards of their hard work and dedication as one of the more popular stops among tourists traveling Historic 66. A visit to the Snow Cap Drive-In, built by Juan and owned by the Delgadillo family, is a must. The drive-in is one of the most photographed and talked-about spots on all of Route 66.

O. C. Osterman Auto Court, Peach Springs
c. 1932

In 1925, former Swedish merchant marine John Osterman sold the gas station he built shortly after World War I to his brother Oscar Osterman. As luck would have it, the primitive road in front of the station was destined to become Highway 66. By 1932, highway improvements relocated the roadway one block north, so Oscar built a new station alongside the road, where it still sits to this day. Oscar utilized the west end of the building as an office and provided a small sleeping quarters for employees over the garage. Shortly after the completion of his new station, Oscar added a row of six small cabins. Business was brisk, and the cabins were paid for by the end of the first summer. To meet demand, he added 16 units with attached garages near the rear of the property.

In 1934, Frank Boyd, disinterested in the farming lifestyle of his native Kansas, left his home to attend college in California. Year after year during the busy summer months he and his brother returned to Peach Springs to work at Osterman's station. After graduating in 1938, Frank decided to settle in Peach Springs. Around the same time, Oscar Osterman, tiring of the auto court, offered the business to Frank, who jumped at the chance. He went to Kansas to collect his new bride, Beatrice, and the couple started their new life together in Peach Springs as owners of O. C. Osterman Auto Court.

Business boomed, especially after World War II, but in 1946, fire destroyed a large portion of their business. They quickly rebuilt and added a gas station to complement the auto court. The bad fortune did not end there. Twenty years later, in 1966, a flood destroyed most of the business. Route 66 entrepreneurs have a certain survivor mentality, and in typical fashion, the Boyds rebuilt everything.

The complex was an operating gas station/convenience store until 2005, but today the service station that Oscar built in 1932 is all that remains of the complex. It now sits closed and empty.

PEACH SPRINGS
c. 1935

Peach Springs is located at the southern tip of the 1-million-acre Hualapai (pronounced *wall-a-pie*) Indian reservation and is home to their tribal headquarters. It was founded in the early 1880s when the Santa Fe Railway established a water station on the site and named it for the peach trees that grow at a nearby spring. It is said that Mormon missionaries planted the trees there while visiting the region in 1852. The onetime western terminus of the Santa Fe Railway located at Peach Springs included a roundhouse, Harvey House restaurant, and a stagecoach line that offered tours to the Grand Canyon beginning in the 1880s.

Prior to 1935, U.S. Highway 66 was a two-lane dirt road through the center of town flanked by a couple of service stations and auto courts. The old tourist courts are long gone, but in their place stands the newly constructed Hualapai Lodge run by the Hualapai tribe. Many improvements were made to the section of road from Seligman through Peach Springs to Hackberry. On the eastern approach to Peach Springs, several of the original sections of Route 66 are visible parallel to the newer version of Route 66. In 1978, Interstate 40 construction on the 70-mile section from Seligman to Kingman was completed, bypassing many small towns along the way including Peach Springs, which was bypassed by 36 miles, the most of any town along the route.

7-V RANCH RESORT, VALENTINE
c. 1935

Ed Carrow began building his multipurpose ranch well before the designation of Highway 66 in 1926. Along with his six brothers, Carrow built up the business that originally consisted of a slaughterhouse and dairy to eventually include a restaurant, garage, gas station, and auto court. The 1924 restaurant on the Old Beale Road was completed from stones that he salvaged from nearby abandoned railroad bridges. The restaurant was a great success, and bus lines made the 7-V Ranch a regular meal stop. A swimming pool was later added, much to the delight of scorched bus passengers, who cooled off with a quick dip before resuming their trips.

Tourist traffic picked up after the designation of Highway 66, and Carrow built a row of eight small cabins to accommodate overnight guests. The cabins were built with two guest units in each building and sat alongside Crozier Creek, which ran through the property. Heavy rains caused the creek to flood in 1939, destroying the garage and gas station. The flood also damaged a portion of the restaurant and some of the cabins. Route 66 was soon rerouted to higher ground to avoid another disaster, thus bypassing the ranch. A few remnants of the 7-V Ranch Resort remain, including the row of cabins alongside Crozier Creek.

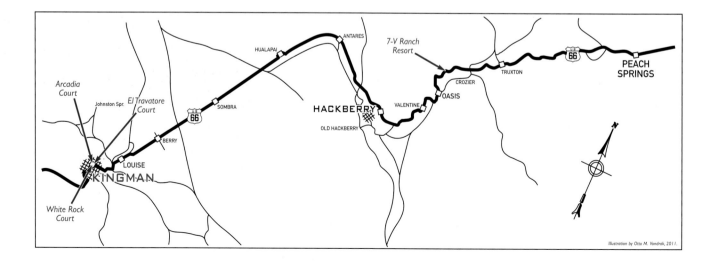

Illustration by Otto M. Vondrak, 2011.

EL TROVATORE COURT, KINGMAN
c. 1960

Since the early 1900s Kingman has served and flourished as an important transportation hub for the western United States. But when Kingman was chosen as a Highway 66 city, the tourist industry began to blossom in earnest, and dozens of auto courts sprang up along Kingman's roadside.

In the late 1930s John F. Miller purchased the future site of the El Trovatore. Miller was no stranger to the hotel business. He built his first in Las Vegas on the corner of Main and Freemont—a two-story structure later known as the Golden Gate Casino—and in December 1939 the El Trovatore received its first guests. The motel consisted of 30 units back in 1939, and overnight rates started at $3 a night. The El Trovatore became a very popular stop in Kingman, and to keep up with demand Miller added another 24 rooms. The bathrooms used hand-cut tiles in a variety of colors to add a very elegant look to each room. A cocktail lounge and dining room were also part of the facility.

The interiors of both were quite unusual, featuring walls lined with large rocks to give the impression of being inside a stone structure.

The interstate bypassed Kingman in 1953, and the El Trovatore subsequently went through a succession of ownership changes. The motel began to slowly deteriorate both in appearance and reputation. In May 2005 Karen M. Kreiger purchased the El Trovatore with plans to revitalize the motel and repair its somewhat seedy reputation. The motel is currently going through a complete renovation; the first phase was completed in 2005 and the second phase, mainly interior renovation, should be completed by April 2006. All rooms will be completely redone by then with new furniture and carpet. Although Kreiger contemplated whether to reopen the El Trovatore as an apartment complex, a motel, or a combination of both, she is leaning toward apartments because of the constant upkeep required for a motel of this size. The rear building is currently in use as monthly rentals.

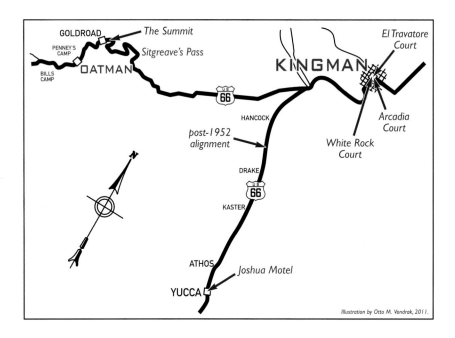

Illustration by Otto M. Vondrak, 2011.

ARCADIA COURT, KINGMAN
c. 1938

In its heyday the Arcadia Court catered to the "well to do." The back of this post card advertises, "Quiet and restful. Luxurious furnishings and the finest appointments for the fastidious guest. Healthiest climate (no humidity) and purest water. Special quarters for chauffeurs and maids." Eventually owners eliminated the garages to make way for more sleeping rooms, and during the early 1950s the Arcadia was remodeled and expanded to include 48 rooms. A heated swimming pool was also added later to keep up with the growing demands of the traveling public. After the Interstates bypassed their towns, many of the historic auto courts along Route 66 began a slow decline. The Arcadia Court was no exception. As motorists blew by Kingman on I-40, the Arcadia Lodge, as it is now known, was left in the dust. Eventually, the classic auto court fell into a state of disrepair and local undesirables began calling the court home. Police were frequent visitors and the fine reputation the Arcadia Court once enjoyed became a distant memory. After a string of disinterested owners, the property was once again sold in 2001. Current managers Frank and Susan Brace are in the process of remodeling all the rooms. The drug dealers and prostitutes are long gone and with the help of the new owner, the Braces hope to once again make the Arcadia a stop of choice for the "fastidious guest."

WHITE ROCK AUTO COURT
14 NEW MODERN CABINS
HI-WAY 66
KINGMAN, ARIZONA

WHITE ROCK COURT, KINGMAN
c. 1935

In 1935, Conrad Minka settled on a narrow plot of land on what was then the east end of Kingman. There he built the White Rock Court out of native tufa stone from a nearby quarry. The unusually bright white stone prompted Conrad to call his business White Rock Court. The guest units were built in two sections laid out in an L shape. Units varied in size, but each of the 14 "modern cabins" had its own covered garage. The two-story main building housed the office and owner's residence. Later, additional guest accommodations were made available on the second story of the office structure.

One unusual aspect of the White Rock Court, especially for tourist facilities of that time, was central heating. This feat was accomplished by building the court over a series of tunnels that connected to a central furnace. Sometime after World War II, the court grew to 22 units. Eventually the stately White Rock Court succumbed to the changing times and was converted to monthly rental units. To make the apartments larger and more attractive, several interior walls separating the individual units were demolished.

Unlike many of the stone-veneered courts along Route 66, the White Rock was completely built of solid stone and masonry. So solid is the construction that if the White Rock structures manage to avoid the strip-mall bulldozer, they will last long into the future, side by side the legacy of Route 66.

KINGMAN
c. 1948

Kingman, located on the gently sloping Hualapai Valley between the Hualapai and Cerbat mountain ranges, began as a railroad siding near Beale's Springs along the newly constructed Atlantic & Pacific Railway. Originally known as Middleton, the name was changed to Kingman in 1882 for Lewis Kingman, a line surveyor on the railroad. The first train pulled into town on March 28, 1883, and Kingman, the little camp by the tracks, has been a major transportation hub for the western states ever since. Kingman flourished during the early 1900s, and many of the buildings constructed then survive today, including the old Brunswick Hotel opened in 1909. Arizona's first commercial airport, Port Kingman, was also opened there in 1929.

Being such an important transportation gateway, it's ironic that most Kingman streets, including Route 66 through town, remained unpaved until around 1940. Stranger still is the fact that until 1941, Kingman was surrounded by fencing to keep wandering livestock off the streets. Kingman has a few Hollywood connections, as well. Clark Gable and Carole Lombard were married at St. John's Methodist church in 1939, and well-known Hollywood entertainer Andy Devine was raised in Kingman; Front Street (Route 66) was changed to Andy Devine Avenue in 1955. In 1953 Interstate 40 was completed in the area, making Kingman one of the first Mother Road cities to be bypassed.

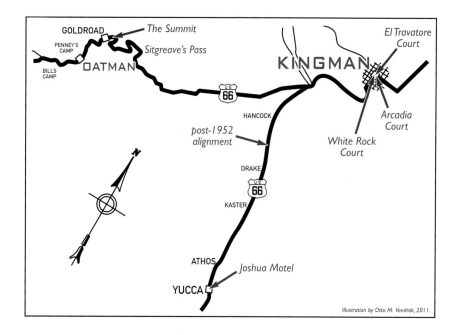

Illustration by Otto M. Vondrak, 2011.

COOL SPRINGS CAMP, KINGMAN
c. 1939

N. R Dunton built the Cool Springs Camp in the Black Mountains on the approach to Sitgreaves Pass in 1927. Being the resourceful person he was, he constructed the original buildings entirely out of stones gathered along the highway. In June 1936 Dunton sold the property to James and Mary Walker from Indiana. The Walker family, including their four children, moved to Cool Springs that summer, and in January 1937, remodeled the business, adding a restaurant and bar. Mary divorced James after a few years and remarried a gentleman named Floyd Spidell, who added a full-service garage and guest cabins, turning the camp into a fully appointed travel stop. Eventually Mary and Floyd divorced and the business was left to Floyd.

The Cool Springs Camp was a very popular destination among travelers, as well as nearby Kingman residents. Well-known for its fabulous chicken dinners, "locals" commuted as far as 20 miles to dine on the famous fowl. The interstate bypassed this dangerous section of Highway 66 in the Black Mountains in 1952 in favor of a straighter and safer route to Topock, Arizona. After the realignment, business slowed to a crawl and the Cool Springs Camp was shut down in 1964 when Floyd packed up and moved to Kingman.

Cool Springs Camp sat closed and mostly forgotten for decades. Vandals slowly destroyed it, and what they did not destroy crumbled and decayed in the unforgiving heat of the desert. For one day in 1991 Cool Springs came to life as a set in the movie *Universal Soldier*. Unfortunately, it was only rebuilt for one purpose: to blow it up for a scene in the movie. The studio eventually moved on, and what they left of Cool Springs was not worth mentioning. There it sat again, a skeleton of what once was a favorite Route 66 roadside eatery among tourists and locals alike.

In 1997 a man named Ned Leuchtner happened to pass through the area and noticed the sparse ruins of Cool Springs. He decided to stop and take a look. The more he dug up, the more he became fascinated with Cool Springs and its colorful history. Researching Cool Spring Camp was fulfilling, but rebuilding the roadside icon became Leuchtner's dream.

He contacted Nancy Waverka, the niece of prior owner Floyd Spidell, and made a few offers, but Waverka refused each, citing sentimental reasons. Leuchtner reassured her that intended to rebuild the camp and eventually gave Waverka the peace of mind she needed to sell. In the summer of 2001 Leuchtner became the overjoyed owner of Cool Springs Camp.

In the fall of 2004 the rebuilding began in earnest. Leuchtner teamed up with general contractor Dennis De Chenne. On December 7, after almost 40 years of darkness, power was hooked up and once again the lights of the Cool Springs Camp lit the night sky. The construction continues. A museum has been proposed where the one-time café building stood, and expansion of the existing gift shop is planned. Although there will be no food service or gasoline, snacks and soft drinks will be sold. With the combined efforts of Leuchtner; site manager De Chenne; and gift-shop manager Betsy Miller and her staff, Judy De Chenne and Lois Cummiskey, the spirit of Cool Springs Camp lives on.

COOLEST
SPOT
ON THE
DESERT

21 miles west
of Kingman,
9 miles east
of Oatman
ARIZONA
on U. S. Hwy. 66

E3910

ED'S CAMP, EAST OF GOLDROAD
c. 1947

Beginning the rugged approach to Sitgreaves Pass from the east, one of the most feared and dreaded sections on all of Route 66, travelers will notice the fading letters of Ed's Camp, spelled out in painted white rocks on the side of a hill. Lowell "Ed" Edgerton purchased the property that Ed's Camp sits on in the late 1930s, hoping to cash in on the ever-increasing flow of tourists. Throughout the 1930s and 1940s, Edgerton expanded his desert oasis to include a grocery store, gas station, trailer camp, and souvenir shop. It was a "camp" in every sense of the word—there were never any cabins or rooms at the site. Motorists on a budget would pull in and sleep in tents or in their cars. For $1, a tired traveler with a little bit of extra

cash could sleep on a cot in a screened porch. Water was an-all-too precious commodity and was sold to guests on a per-bucket basis unless they paid the buck to spend the night—then it was free.

Edgerton went on to become a world-renowned figure in the field of geology. Amateur geologists came from around the world to hunt the area for precious stones, paying Edgerton a small fee for the privilege. In 1952, Route 66 was realigned around the Black Mountains from Kingman to Topock, bypassing the steep and treacherous mountain pass. Ed died in 1978, but his camp remains, for all intents and purposes undisturbed and hearkening back to better days.

THE SUMMIT, SITGREAVES PASS
c. 1940

As it scales the foreboding Black Mountains, Highway 66 rises to a peak of 3,550 feet above sea level between Kingman and Oatman. The pass through this mountain range was named for Captain Lorenzo Sitgreaves, who in 1851 was sent on a mission to assess the navigability of the Zuni and Colorado rivers for use in a possible confrontation with the Mormon settlement in Utah. Around 1861 Sitgreaves Pass was the site of an emigrant massacre by the Hualapi and Mohave Indians.

The Summit filling station and ice cream parlor was located 24 miles west of Kingman, on the first routing of Route 66 through the Black Mountains at the summit of Sitgreaves Pass. Imagine inching up the pass in your automobile. The car has no air conditioning, and as hot as it is outside, it is hotter in the car. The gas gauge is reading low.

You should have listened to your wife and filled up earlier. The kids are complaining every step of the way. Your throats are parched. As the car struggles on, beads of sweat fall from your forehead, clouding your vision. As you reach the summit you are just able to make out a sign up ahead on the right. Does that sign say "Ice Cream"? No, it couldn't be. Ice cream and beer? The kids see the ice cream sign and demand you pull over. Of course you were going to anyway. This scene probably occurred several times a day on this section of Route 66. The Summit must have been a strange and wonderful sight after taking on the perils of the pass.

Today memories of relieved parents and children's faces dripping with ice cream as well as a few crumbling foundations are all that are left of the Summit, which burned to the ground in 1967.

350

TOPOCK
c. 1941

Topock began in 1883 as a small settlement populated by bridge builders and railroad employees who were constructing the first bridge across this section of the Colorado River. The area was chosen for the crossing because of the narrow width of the river at this point. When a post office was established in 1906, the settlement was originally called Acme, but later changed to Topock, a native American word for "water crossing."

There is no real town of Topock, and to give you an idea how little there is here, the Topock post office is actually located in the nearby community of Golden Shores. The Needles Ferry was established here in 1890 and was the only way to cross the river if you were not traveling by rail. The ferry continued to carry travelers across the Colorado until a flood destroyed the facility in 1914. *A Guidebook to Highway 66* (1946) states that Topock's facilities at that time included "gas, grocery, a few cabins, and a garage for light repairs; limited facilities." Nothing remains of these "limited facilities," although there is a marina on the shores of the Colorado River.

JOSHUA MOTEL, YUCCA
c. 1954

Prior to October 1952, Route 66 left Kingman and wound its way up and around the Black Mountains over Sitgreaves Pass on through Oatman to the shores of the Colorado River at Topock, Arizona. Although a beautiful mountain desert drive, the windy, serpentine roadway was quite hazardous, with a propensity for major backups and delays. October 1, 1952, saw that all come to an end. The new alignment of Route 66 went around the Black Mountains, bypassing Oatman and the treacherous mountain terrain. This cut several miles and hours off travel time from Kingman to the border of California. Route 66 was now a straight shot from Kingman to Topock with not much in between except for desert and the small town of Yucca situated 25 miles west of Kingman.

During World War II, Yucca was home to the Yucca Army Airfield. The Ford Motor Company purchased the land in 1954 and built a vehicle test facility that is still in operation today.

Yucca blossomed in the years following the realignment of Route 66. Several motels and cafés were built to serve the insurgence of travelers now coming through town. One of these new motels was built on the south side of Route 66 and was known as the Joshua Motel, offering tubs, showers, refrigerators, vented heat, and free TV in rooms connected to a café.

Yucca's growth, however, was short lived. In the 1970s, the interstate covered most of the roadway from Kingman to Topock. Yucca slowly faded as the parade of cars and onetime customers whizzed by on the interstate. Westbound travelers stopped short in Kingman while eastbound travelers drove the extra 25 miles to Kingman for its larger selection of motels and cafés.

CAFE **THE OUTPOST** NOVELTY

CALIFORNIA

In the 1930s, countless Dust Bowl families left the drought-plagued heartland in search of a better life. The Great Depression was also in full swing and Route 66 to California was the escape route of choice. These early travelers who braved Sitgreaves Pass and perilous sections in Arizona must have first been disappointed in their destination. After crossing the Colorado River, expecting a glimpse of rich and fertile land filled with blossoming orange groves, they found more desert.

The first town after crossing the Colorado was Needles, where summer temperatures can soar to 125 degrees Fahrenheit. Imagine piling all your worldly possessions on an old Ford, tires barely keeping the rims from grinding on pavement, leaving all you knew behind, and suffering incredible heat and hardships, only to find more of what you just left behind. The Mojave Desert between Needles and Barstow, 150 blistering miles via the early alignment, was some of the most treacherous road on all of Route 66. Tiny hamlets along this stretch provided motorists with not much more than the essentials. Throughout Route 66's history, wrecker services along this section worked 24 hours a day, picking up stranded motorists or towing the really unlucky ones involved in accidents. During World War II the region was used by Patton to train his troops for battle against the Germans in North Africa.

Veterans of this blistering stretch of Route 66 knew to travel by night and to carry plenty of water. Once they reached Barstow, most Dust Bowl families left the Mother Road and headed north toward Bakersfield, hoping to find work in the farmlands of the San Joaquin Valley. Travel from Barstow to Los Angeles was relatively worry-free compared to the desert crossing, but not without its own perils. The Cajon Pass, "Gateway to Southern California," posed a formidable challenge as it wound its way down a difficult grade to San Bernardino. From there, 66 sliced through Upland, Azusa, Duarte, Arcadia, and Pasadena. The original western terminus of Route 66 was the intersection of Broadway and 7th Street in downtown Los Angeles. On January 1, 1936, the route was extended through Hollywood to Santa Monica, where it took a left-hand turn on to Lincoln Boulevard and ended at the intersection with Olympic Boulevard. Contrary to popular belief, Route 66 never reached the Santa Monica Pier or the Pacific Ocean.

Los Angeles saw so many alignment changes over the years that a complete guidebook, *Route 66 in Los Angeles County* by Scott R Piotrowski, was dedicated to unraveling its mysteries. One notable realignment, the Arroyo Seco Parkway, was considered the first freeway west of the Mississippi. Construction was completed on the Parkway in the late 1940s, and it is listed as a National Scenic Byway.

Whether you were a migrant family fleeing the Dust Bowl, an unemployed factory worker looking for a better life during the Great Depression, an actor dreaming of making it big in Hollywood, or simply taking the family on its annual summer vacation, reaching California was the collective dream and U.S. Highway 66 was the bright beacon that helped guide the masses and transform those dreams into reality.

TRAILS ARCH BRIDGE
AND RED ROCK BRIDGE
c. 1933

The first bridge to cross the Colorado River at Topock was a wooden structure built by the railroad in 1883. In 1890 the Phoenix Bridge Company built one of the first steel bridges in the country, the Red Rock Bridge, to replace the outdated wooden bridge for the Atlantic & Pacific Railroad. With a construction cost of almost a half million dollars, the Red Rock Bridge was thought to be excessive and very expensive at the time. Trains quickly became heavier and stressed the limits of the new steel bridge. Modifications were needed to strengthen the structure, first in 1901, then again in 1911.

If you were not traveling by train, crossing the Colorado was a different story. Prior to the automobile, the Needles Ferry carried horse and foot traffic across the Colorado beginning in 1890. When the automobile appeared on the scene, this ferry served motor traffic traveling the Old National Trails Highway. In 1914 a massive flood took out the ferry service, leaving travelers stranded on both sides of the river. Wooden planks were laid over the railroad ties of the bridge. Motorists were allowed to cross between trains, as railroad employees with train schedules in hand coordinated the crossings.

The Red Rock Bridge continued to carry automobile traffic until the Old Trails Arch Bridge was completed on February 20, 1916. The first alignment of Route 66 crossed the Colorado River from Topock, Arizona, to Needles, California (14 miles to the west) via this bridge, seen in the background of the postcard and photograph. The Old Trails Arch Bridge carried the dirt path of the National Old Trails Highway for more than 10 years prior to the designation of U.S. Highway 66 in 1926. Located about 800 feet downstream of the Red Rock Bridge, the Old Trails Arch Bridge was a marvel in its own right. For 12 years it stood as the longest three-hinged arch bridge in the country.

Although it was quite the engineering accomplishment at the time, the bridge had its limitations. The load limit was only 11 tons, and the roadbed was so narrow that bus and truck traffic were able to cross only one way at a time. A warning sign was posted at both ends of the bridge to help avoid head-on collisions: "One Way for Trucks and Buses." This restriction proved quite annoying to motorists from time to time, but for the most part traffic was light enough and did not pose serious problems until later years.

With the coming of World War II, truck traffic on all of America's highways increased dramatically. This increase, along with the growing size of vehicles, spelled the beginning of the end for the Old Trails Arch Bridge. Automobile travel and truck traffic continued to grow by leaps and bounds, especially in the years immediately following World War II. The graceful old bridge was no longer able to handle the heavy traffic load that Highway 66 now supported. A new automobile crossing over the Colorado was desperately needed.

In 1945 the Santa Fe Railway established a new river crossing, opening the possibility for auto traffic to once again flow over the Red Rock Bridge. It was determined that an adequate crossing was already in place and a new bridge did not need to be built. The rails and ties were removed from the Red Rock Bridge and concrete was poured for the roadbed. On May 21, 1947, the Red Rock Railroad Bridge conversion was complete, and automobile traffic once again flowed over the venerable bridge. When the new four-lane steel bridge carrying Interstate 40 was completed in 1966, the Red Rock Bridge was unceremoniously closed and remained abandoned until it was completely dismantled in 1976. Only the concrete pilings remain.

The Old Trails Arch Bridge, once in danger of the same fate, was again put to use and today carries a natural gas pipeline from Texas for the Pacific Gas and Electric Company. For a nice look at the Old Trails Arch Bridge in its heyday, watch the Joads cross it in the movie version of John Steinbeck's novel *The Grapes of Wrath*.

TOPOC AND SANTA FE RAILWAY BRIDGES OVER COLORADO RIVER, NEAR NEEDLES, CAL.

CARTY'S CAMP, NEEDLES
c. 1931

While visiting the Grand Canyon, Santa Fe Railway employee Bill Carty stayed in a cabin that was something of a tent/cabin hybrid. Upon his return to Needles, he enthusiastically brought up the idea of starting a tourist camp and auto court to a friend and coworker, one Mr. Manskar. Manskar thought it was a great idea to open an auto camp in Needles, and in 1925 Carty's Camp became a reality. Both the Carty and Manskar families were involved in operating the facility, and both lived on the premises for a time. Manskar grew weary of the business, though, and Carty eventually bought out his interest. Carty quit his position at the railroad to manage the business full time.

The facility eventually expanded to include a gas station, garage, cottages, campground, and a motel, which Carty dubbed Havasu Court. Havasu Court consisted of 12 cabins, each with an attached garage, in two back-to-back rows. Shade in Needles is gold, especially in the summer months when temperatures can climb into the high 120s, and a small, shaded picnic area located directly across from the camp was a favorite among customers. Carty's Camp flourished and became the place to stay in Needles.

Carty retired from the business in 1948 and sold the camp to Charles Canterbury and Loren Armes. Both the Canterbury and Armes families shared the day-to-day operations, and, like their predecessors, both families lived on-site. Mildred Armes remembers Route 66 as a gold mine that provided customers from 6 a.m. to 10 p.m. every day. "We worked our tails off," she was quoted as saying. The two families also built and operated a gas station in Needles called the C&A Chevron Gas Station, which included a lunchroom and store. Eventually the families retired from the business, and the camp closed shortly thereafter. Not much is left of the remaining structures, on which the desert climate has taken its toll. Today a few of the cabins are used for storage.

Carty's Camp was a true reflection of what auto travel on early Highway 66 was all about. The Joad family passed in front of Carty's in the screen version of *The Grapes of Wrath*. That appearance in itself makes the site of Carty's Camp hallowed grounds. Just standing on the property, one hearkens back to the days of early auto travel when excitement, adventure, and even danger were part of an automobile trip. That real sense of adventure is captured on a note written on the back of a postcard dated June 24, 1931: "Dear Daddie, It is now 11:55 p.m. We are going on across the desert tonight. It is very hot and dry. We will write when we get on the other side. Love Florence."

THE PALMS MOTEL, NEEDLES
c. 1946

Needles was always an important stop along Highway 66. For westbound travelers, it was the jumping-off point for crossing the treacherous Mojave. Those headed east and emerging from the Mojave took a deep breath, gave a sigh of relief, and thanked their lucky stars to have made it without incident.

The Palms Motel is located on the eastern edge of town where Broadway and Front Street split. The motel's origins date to the 1920s, when it was located on the west edge of town. In the motel business they say location is everything, and the cabins were eventually moved to their current location in the late 1930s. Prior to the move, the eastern location was the site of a tent camp for the railroad, and the Palms soon became a favorite sleepover for railroad employees.

Along with Carty's Camp, the Palms Motel was one of the first tourist facilities that weary westbound travelers saw when approaching Needles. Operated by Guy and Orsavella Austin in its early days, it consisted of 14 units, 8 of which had kitchen facilities.

The Palms has gone through a succession of owners. In 1991 Hank and Edna Wilde purchased the property from Luis Bravo and transformed the motel into a bed and breakfast renamed the Old Trails Inn. The B&B never really took off, and it closed in 1997. Bravo reacquired the property and proceeded to fully renovate each unit. The walls were stripped bare, and new plumbing and wiring were installed throughout the property. The Palms currently has 16 units, all of which are rented monthly.

NEEDLES
c. 1929

The town of Needles was established in 1883 as a burgeoning railroad town and mining hub. To this day the railroad is by far its largest employer. Known as "The Gateway to California," Needles got its name from the jagged, sharply pointed peaks of the Black Mountains southwest of the town. To say that it gets hot in this part of the country is a major understatement. Jack Rittenhouse, author of 1946's *A Guide Book to Highway 66:* "In the hot months, it is advisable to make the drive from Needles to Barstow, over the Mojave Desert, either in the evening, night or early morning hours. In any case, it is advisable to carry extra water for the car."

Needles is home to the ornate El Garces, a onetime Harvey House that served railroad customers until 1949. Today, the Friends of El Garces hope to restore the magnificent structure for future generations to enjoy. In 1973 Interstate 40 was completed and tourist traffic fell dramatically as cars disappeared. A few of the classic motels and cafés survive, but that's a relative term. In this part of the country, Route 66 was born out of crude dirt pathways and wooden-plank roads that twisted their way across the desert. The onetime concrete artery that fed life into the western part of our nation is slowly and begrudgingly returning to that desert, as America's Main Street begins its gradual decay and the Mojave slowly reclaims its own.

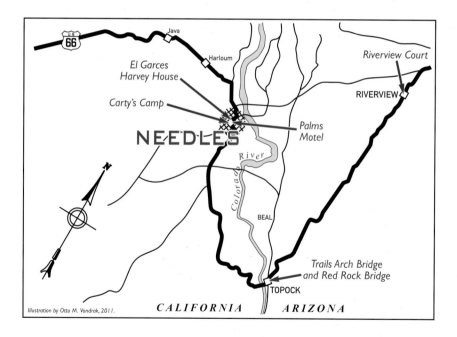

EL GARCES HARVEY HOUSE, NEEDLES
c. 1927

During the golden age of rail travel, the names Santa Fe and Fred Harvey went hand in hand. The enterprising Mr. Harvey began his relationship with the Atchison, Topeka & Santa Fe Railway in 1878, and by 1889, he had struck a deal for exclusive rights to operate lunchrooms and hotels at Santa Fe train depots west of the Missouri River. The first Harvey House was built in Topeka, Kansas, and opened in 1876. At the peak of his business, Fred Harvey operated 84 Harvey Houses that served rail customers, as well as automobile travelers in later years.

Many Harvey Houses were located in key Route 66 towns. Needles, California, has always been an important stop prior to taking on the challenges of the brutal Mojave Desert. No Harvey House was more prominent and elegant than the El Garces in downtown Needles. Construction of the El Garces began in 1906 following a fire that destroyed the original wooden depot. Not wanting a repeat fire, Harvey decided the new depot would be built entirely of concrete. The primary labor force used in the construction came from the region's Mojave Indian population who handled many of the more hazardous jobs. Construction and landscaping of this most elegant Harvey House was completed in 1908, and it has played an integral part in the community ever since. Because the El Garces was built to serve rail passengers, the side facing the tracks is the more ornate side. Standing trackside, despite its present condition, the former elegance of this grand old lady is still evident.

The El Garces was considered the crown jewel of the entire chain and was well-known throughout the country for its fine food and lodging. This Harvey House not only served rail passengers—the local community took advantage of these fine facilities as well. The El Garces, named for Father Francisco Garces, a Catholic missionary who came to the area in 1776, played host to countless private parties, weddings, and banquets. Guests of the El Garces were treated with fine china, silverware, and real Irish linens, as well as fresh flowers daily. A sample dinner menu might consist of red snapper, Long Island duckling, and fresh Bluepoint oysters with fresh vegetables. Crème puffs and chocolate éclairs for dessert were standard fare. The food was served by well-trained waitresses, known as Harvey Girls, who received intense training.

Elegant dining rooms were not the only place to dine at the El Garces. A lunchroom and soda fountain were also part of the facility, allowing travelers to leave the train. In the lunchroom, Harvey Girls worked two large U-shaped counters serving up "train specials." Service was quick, allowing travelers time to reboard. When travel by automobile began its rise in popularity, the El Garces served travelers braving the primitive dirt path of the National Old Trails Highway that ran in front of the depot. The National Old Trails Highway gave way to U.S. Highway 66 in 1926, and the elegant Harvey House continued its fine tradition of serving the traveling public.

The Harvey Girls lived on the second floor. Room and board and clean uniforms were provided as part of their salary, which could be as much as $17.50 per month. So attractive were the Harvey Girls, it is said that many a rail worker would scamper onto the roofs of the railcars when pulling into the El Garces, hoping to catch a glimpse of these beautiful women relaxing outside their second-floor dormitory.

One of the major problems of operating a luxury hotel and restaurant in an arid desert location such as Needles is the oppressive heat during the summer months. The temperature often climbs into the mid-120-degree range. The heat problem was solved for El Garces when an ice plant was built nearby. Each day 1,080 blocks of ice, weighing in at a hefty 300 pounds each, were made. To cool the El Garces, refrigerator cars were lined up on the tracks and filled with ice. An array of pipes and blowers circulated air through the ice-filled cars. This icy cool air was then routed through shafts buried under the tracks that led into the depot, cooling the entire facility. About every four days the cars were refilled with ice. The ice from the plant was also used to keep perishables fresh during rail transport across country.

As rail travel began a sharp decline during the 1940s, the El Garces felt the pinch and closed as a Harvey House in 1949. The facility was utilized as offices for the Santa Fe Railway until 1988. After its closing, the Harvey House fell victim to vandalism and the ravages of time. In 1993, the Friends of El Garces (www.friendsofelgarces.org) formed with the purpose of restoring the historic train depot. It is hoped the El Garces will one day reopen with a California Visitor's Welcoming Center, a Friends of El Garces exhibit, and railroad museum.

MOUNTAIN SPRINGS AUTO CAMP, MOUNTAIN SPRINGS
c. 1940

Upon leaving Needles, the desert quickly became a formidable adversary to traveler and automobile alike. Traveling westward from Needles in the day during the hot summer months was not recommended and only attempted by the brave or foolhardy. Mountain Springs Auto Camp was located only 27 miles west of Needles but probably felt more like 270 miles to the daring daytime motorist. For 27 miles, Highway 66 made a steady climb from an altitude of 483 feet above sea level in Needles to 2,700 feet at Mountain Springs. There the traveler was faced with another 135 blistering desert miles to the nearest sizeable town of Barstow.

Motorists would spend the day in Mountain Springs preparing for the harsh desert crossing. Don't forget extra water. The camp comprised a few cabins, a lunchroom, a gas station, and a small garage. Did I mention the extra water? As with a majority of desert stops on this section of Route 66, water was at a premium. Trucks hauled in the precious cargo, and unless you bought gasoline, you were charged for it by the gallon. This undoubtedly was the cause of many "heated" arguments between owner and motorist. Once billed as the "coolest spot on the desert," Mountain Springs Auto Camp was obliterated by the arrival of the interstate.

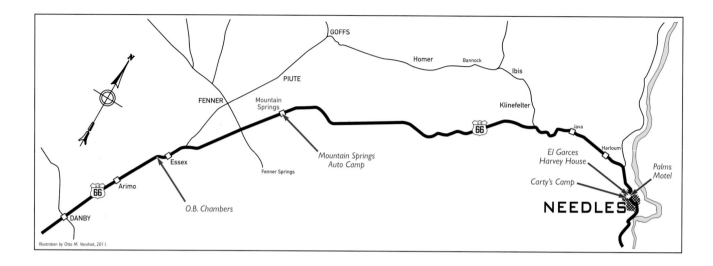

Illustration by Otto M. Vondrak, 2011.

ESSEX
c. 1942

It is rumored that the tiny Mojave Desert town of Essex was founded when an unlucky motorist broke down in the area. With no towing or service station for miles, he decided to stay and call this desert spot home. Being an enterprising sort, he opened a towing service with a café, and Essex was born, located on a section of road originally known as the National Old Trails Highway. In 1926 this road was redesignated U.S. Highway 66. During the late 1940s and the 1950s, Essex offered travelers and tourists all the essentials needed for desert travel, including towing services, gasoline, food, and water. Back in the days when tourist traffic regularly flowed through town, clean water was a precious commodity sold to

motorists at 10 cents per glass for drinking; unfiltered water was sold at 10 cents per gallon for car radiators. The Automobile Club of Southern California graciously installed a free drinking fountain in town, alleviating the outrageous charges levied by local businesses. This stone well-like structure still stands a couple of hundred feet from the onetime market and just a few feet south of the highway. Although no longer in service, it reminds us of the dangers that once confronted early motorists traveling the Mojave. The U.S. Postal Service is the only remaining Essex business still in operation. The café was reopened sometime in the 1990s but was eventually shut down and remains abandoned.

O. B. CHAMBERS MOTEL-CAFÉ-SERVICE STATION, ESSEX
c. 1959

The desert has a knack for forever hiding its encounters with human civilization. Left unattended, even the hardiest structures will fall to the harsh elements of the Mojave. Located 41 miles west of Needles, the O. B. Chambers tourist stop is one such example. This business' only link to the present is found in this advertising postcard and possibly in the memories of a few still-living customers who once stopped for gas and refreshment.

The business was originally established in the mid-1930s and subsequently rebuilt in the late 1930s after being totally destroyed by fire. According to J. R. Bentley, who moved to Essex in the 1940s and owns a nearby truck tire shop, Chambers arrived in Essex at the end of World War II. Chambers bought the place and built it up to a full-service tourist facility that included a café, several "modern air-cooled" cabins, and a service station. Throughout the 1950s and into the 1960s, the business flourished as vehicles flowed through town, energizing the local economy. By the late 1960s, the business closed, never to reopen. The desert immediately began its slow consumption of the abandoned structures, and in 1975, as reported by Bentley, all remaining traces of O. B. Chambers' facility were razed.

Essex was never a town in the true sense. It was built out of necessity—a desert oasis created simply to care for the traveling masses. This is evident in the simple text on the back of the postcard, which reads, "Population 24 (including dogs) Phone: Essex 1."

CADIZ SUMMIT SERVICE, CADIZ
c. 1946

Cadiz Summit Service was originally built in the 1920s by George and Minnie Tienken on the old alignment of U.S. Highway 66 that ran through Goffs and Fenner, California. In 1931, Route 66 was realigned from Goffs to create a straighter, more direct path. Undaunted, George and Minnie moved the business, buildings and all, to this new location about 18 miles west of Essex. After a long, hot, and often hazardous summer day's travel in the Mojave, this lonely California rest stop must have been a very welcome site. Standing in the now-deserted parking area, one can almost see and hear the hustle and bustle of hot and thirsty travelers looking for a cold drink or a quick snack.

Interstate 40 bypassed this section of Route 66 in 1972, cutting off its lifeblood and allowing another landmark roadside business to fall victim to the name of progress. Soon after the bypass, traffic along the route slowed to a trickle and Cadiz Summit closed its doors. In no time, vandals and looters took over and a fire finally destroyed what was left. Jack Rittenhouse, in his *Guide Book to Highway 66,* wrote of Cadiz Summit, "a handful of tourist cabins, a café and gas station comprise this desert oasis." No visible evidence of the cabins remains.

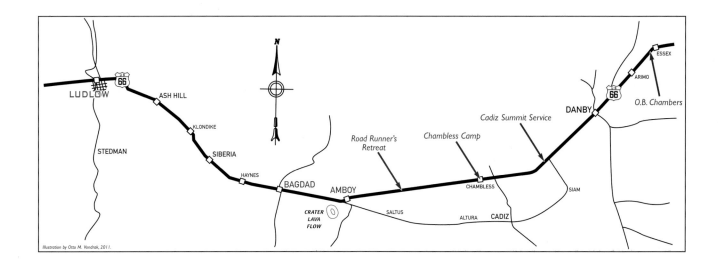

Illustration by Otto M. Vondrak, 2011.

CHAMBLESS CAMP, CHAMBLESS
c. 1932

In the 1920s a widower named James A. Chambless, along with his two children, relocated from Arkansas to the Amboy, California, area. In 1932 he built the small Chambless Camp out of handmade blocks, hoping to cash in on the burgeoning auto-tourist trade. He quickly expanded the business into a full-service stop that included a service station, café, grocery, and cabins. The main building, housing the grocery and service station, featured a large canopy over the pumps to provide shade to customers while they were filling up. Jack D. Rittenhouse, in his 1946 book, *A Guidebook to Highway 66*, describes the Chambless Camp as "one of the few shady spots in the entire desert route."

Much of the business relied on first-time desert travelers who unknowingly attempted to cross the desert during the heat of the day. Wreckers were at the ready, mechanics were on duty, the café was open to feed stranded travelers, and cabins were available for overnight stays if repairs were extensive. Sometime in the late 1930s, Chambless was remarried to a woman named Fannie Gould.

She took over the reins of the business and turned the Chambless Camp into a virtual desert oasis, adding, among other things, a fishpond and a sprawling rose garden, both very unusual sights in this region of the Mojave Desert. In addition, a picnic area lined with acacia trees provided shade and added the oasis-like feel of the grounds.

The early 1970s saw the opening of Interstate 40, and most businesses along this stretch of Highway 66 soon closed. Sometime in the early 1990s, the canopy over the gasoline pumps at the Chambless Camp was destroyed in a violent windstorm, and more recently the pumps were removed. Gus Lizalde bought the property in the early 1990s and planned to renovate the camp to include a Mexican restaurant, a remodeled service station, and RV hookups. The restaurant was open for a time, but the rest of the renovations never really got off the ground. The old cabins still stand and are rented to workers who farm the vineyards in nearby Cadiz. The majority of the property remains abandoned and is, inch by inch, being slowly reclaimed by the harsh desert elements.

ROAD RUNNER'S RETREAT, EAST AMBOY
c. 1960

Located 9 miles east of Amboy and a short half mile west of the Chambless Camp, the Road Runner's Retreat was a relative latecomer along Route 66 in this part of the Mojave, opening sometime in the mid- to late 1950s. The restaurant served classic road food and was an extremely popular stop for truckers. The interstate bypassed this section of Highway 66 in the early 1970s, leaving most of the businesses from Essex to Ludlow, including the Road Runner's Retreat, high and dry.

In 1988 the Road Runner's Retreat received a face-lift when Dodge decided to film a television commercial on the site. For a couple of days the gas station and restaurant once again jumped with the hustle and bustle of people coming and going. The clamor of cars pulling in and out of the gas station and restaurant must have truly been a strange sight for the local wildlife. Then, just as suddenly as the silence was broken, order was restored, and the wild creatures and birds reinhabited the empty structures. It is stunning how loud the quiet is here and how much of an outsider humans truly are. As a light breeze breaks the silence and makes its way through the hollow buildings, perhaps a faint sound, barely audible, can be heard— maybe it's a friendly "Beep beep."

ROY'S MOTEL/CAFÉ, AMBOY
c. 1959

In 1938, Roy Crowl, his wife Velma, and their two children, Lloyd and Betty, opened a garage and service station in Amboy. In 1938, Buster Burris rolled into town and went to work for Roy, driving Roy's tow truck. Buster's plan was to stay a short while, make some money, and leave. What he did not plan on was falling in love with Roy's daughter, Betty, and getting married. Buster grew to love not only Betty, but also the desert. Buster and Betty decided to stay, and by the early 1940s, Roy and Buster became partners.

In 1945, Buster added a café to Roy's complex, hoping to cash in on hungry tourists waiting to get their cars fixed in his garage. By 1948, six small cabins accommodated customers who needed to stay overnight while waiting for repairs to be completed. Eventually business became so good that Buster added a 2-story, 18-unit building in the back to meet demand.

During Amboy's heyday in the 1950s, the town supported three restaurants, three service stations, a train depot, and a bus station. Roy's was open 24/7 and was a madhouse. Of the 700-plus Amboy residents, 90 were employed full-time at Roy's. During the peak summer months that number reached as high as 120. The iconic Roy's Motel/Café sign was erected on February 1, 1959, and is a recognized worldwide as a symbol of the halcyon days of Route 66.

In 1972, Interstate 40 cut off traffic to Amboy, severely affecting business. Most folks fled after the bypass, but Roy and Buster kept hanging on. In 1977, Roy passed away, leaving Buster to operate the business. Sometime in the late 1970s, Buster's wife, Betty, died. Buster remarried a woman named Bessie in 1982 who used the motel's lobby as a showcase and gallery for her paintings and pottery.

In 1995, Buster and Bessie called it quits and moved to nearby Twenty-Nine Palms to retire. That same year the town was leased to Walt Wilson, a restaurateur, and Tim White, a New York photographer. In 2000, after the lease expired, Wilson and White purchased the town from Buster for $710,000. Buster died shortly after the sale.

In 2003, Wilson and White offered the complete town on eBay for one month with an asking price of $1.9 million. The highest bid was $995,000. Bessie regained ownership when Wilson and White were unable to meet the payment schedule and the town went into foreclosure.

On May 3, 2005, Amboy was sold to Albert Okura, owner of the Juan Pollo restaurant chain, for an unconfirmed amount of $425,000. Okura plans to restore the café, gas station, and motel to their original working status.

HIGHWAY "66" AMBOY, CALIF. 344

AMBOY
c. 1946

Both Herman "Buster" Burris and Roy Crowl figure prominently in Amboy's growth during the glory days of Route 66. A native Texan, Burris was working as a mechanic at the nearby March Air Base when he met and married Crowl's daughter. He and Crowl went on to become business partners. In 1940 Burris opened a repair shop and in 1945 a café. A couple of cabins were also built to accommodate customers waiting for repairs. In 1948 he began construction on a motel that was completed in its present form in 1952. The famous "Roy's Motel" sign was built in 1959 and remains one of the most recognizable structures on all of Route 66.

"I used to think everybody in the world was driving through Amboy," said Burris. The town's population grew at a frantic pace as mechanics, waitresses, and motel help moved to the area. When Interstate 40 bypassed Amboy in the 1970s, "It was just like somebody put up a gate across Route 66. The traffic just plain stopped," recalled Burris. Through the years Burris expanded the business as opportunities arose, until one day he found he owned the whole town. In the early 1980s he put the complete town up for sale. The asking price: $350,000. Walt Wilson and Timothy White purchased Amboy in 2000 and rented the town out as a film location. In 2002 Amboy was once again put up for sale, this time on eBay, but the reserve price was not met and Amboy remains unsold.

BAGDAD
c. 1950s

The desert town of Bagdad began in 1883 as a small railroad stop. When the Orange Blossom and Lady Lou mines struck pay dirt around the turn of the century, the town of Bagdad became a major gold shipping point. As the mining industry declined, so did Bagdad's fortunes. In 1923 the town lost its post office and by 1937 the mines were closing at a rapid pace, but the Santa Fe depot remained to transport ore, and Bagdad continued to be a coal and water stop for steam engines.

By the 1940s most of the mines were closed and Bagdad, whose population once peaked at close to 600, dropped to about 20. Still, business from Route 66 traffic kept some of the town alive. Paul Limon, a onetime gas station attendant remembers, "Bagdad was a lively little place. People from all over the desert would come here because of the Bagdad Café, owned and operated by a woman named Alice Lawrence. The Bagdad Café was the only place for miles around with a dance floor and jukebox." The café, gas station, cabins, and market continued to serve travelers until 1972, when the Interstate opened to the north. The 1988 film *Bagdad Café,* inspired by the town and its café, was actually filmed in Newberry Springs, 50 miles west of Bagdad. In 1991 the site was used as storage for a natural gas project and the town was wiped clean. Today, there is no evidence the town ever existed.

LUDLOW
c. 1940

"In comparison with neighboring towns, Ludlow is a metropolis," read the 1939 WPA guide to U.S. Highway 66 in California. The population of Ludlow, including railroad crews' families and miners who worked the nearby Bagdad Chase Mines, reached a peak of about 150. Established in 1882, the town was named for William B. Ludlow, who repaired railcars for the nearby Santa Fe Railway. This area of the Mojave was so isolated that the Santa Fe had to import water in tanker cars. The water was then pumped into an elevated storage tank and gravity fed to Ludlow's thirsty residents until 1965 when Ludlow's first

well was dug. The Murphy Brothers Mercantile Store was the most prominent business, along with a "mall" consisting of a pool hall/tavern, grocery store, and restaurant that served locals and travelers alike. When Route 66 was the main artery to the West, Ludlow enjoyed a booming travel business. That ended when Interstate 40 bypassed the town in 1972, marking Ludlow's second economic collapse, the first being the decline of mining in the 1940s. Today, Ludlow consists of a couple of service stations, a café, and a motel to serve the needs of Interstate travelers and Route 66 explorers.

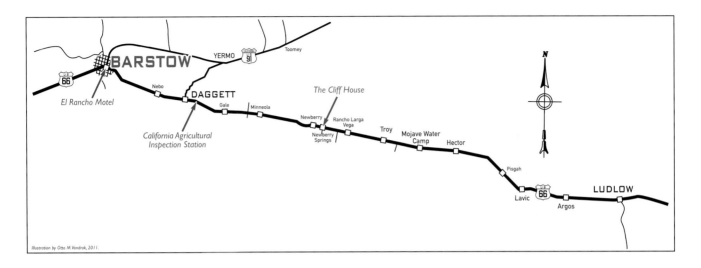

Illustration by Otto M. Vondrak, 2011.

THE CLIFF HOUSE, NEWBERRY SPRINGS
c. 1929

The area known as Newberry Springs began to see its first permanent settlers in the 1880s. Newberry Springs is located on an ancient lakebed covering a large basin of underground water. In its early days, the area was simply and aptly known as Water. It provided the eastern Mojave with a steady supply of water and was the main source used by the railroad in the region. By 1911, the area was known as Newberry, and by 1967, it was Newberry Springs. (The change was prompted by the U.S. Postal Service when mail for Newberry kept turning up in a California city by the name of Newberry Park.)

The Cliff House was built around 1930 with a gas station, café, and six rental cabins. The Cliff House also contained the post office and general store, and was a stop for both the Greyhound and Continental Trailways bus lines. In 1939, a public swimming pool was built, much to the delight of everyone in the region. The Cliff House became the center for community activities for many years as well as a popular meeting spot for teenagers and children in the area.

Besides the pool, another reason the Cliff House became a community hub was that, until the mid-1950s, it had the only telephone in the region. An old wooden box phone complete with hand-crank hung on the wall of the Cliff House, alerting residents of a call with a one long and one short ring sequence.

Nothing private in these parts.

During the golden years of Highway 66, Newberry had an abundance of tourist facilities, including five gas stations, four motels, four garages, and five cafés.

Today, the Cliff House pool is as dry as the surrounding sand and the cabins are long gone. The main building has changed hands and uses several times. Today it is known as Deel Plumbing Heating. Newberry Springs is much quieter these days and has little in the way of tourist services except for a gas station and convenience store near the interstate exit. Oh, and most everyone now has his or her own phone.

CALIFORNIA AGRICULTURAL INSPECTION STATION, DAGGETT
c. 1953

This California Agricultural Inspection Station was built in 1953 and was the third of three such stations built in Daggett. Agricultural inspection stations were set up all around California in an effort to prevent the import and transport of diseased fruits and plants and harmful parasites. These searches prevented fast-moving diseases and parasites from devastating entire crops and so protected the state's large, important citrus and vegetable industries. All westbound traffic was stopped, and each car was given a complete and thorough search. Plants, fruits, and vegetables were quickly confiscated, and incoming motorists were then given an inspection and admission certificate allowing them to pass.

Interstate 40 eventually replaced Route 66 in the area, and the Daggett station was permanently shut down in 1967. (The current inspection station sits on the super-slab just outside of Needles.) The second of the three inspection stations was built in 1930 and is the one seen in the 1940 movie version of *The Grapes of Wrath*. Sadly, during the 1930s, these inspection stations and dozens of makeshift stations around the state were often used to weed out "undesirables" as thousands fled the choking, dust-ridden plains of the Midwest. Thousands of people were turned away when inspectors deemed them unfit to pass. It is said that many of these displaced Okies and Arkies, without the means to satisfy inspectors—and virtually stripped of all hope for a future—walked despondently into the desert, never to be seen again.

EL RANCHO MOTEL, BARSTOW
c. 1947

A man named Cliff Chase built the El Rancho Motel in 1947 entirely from old railroad ties salvaged from the Tonopah & Tidewater Railroad. During the heyday of Route 66, Barstow became an essential stop for travelers arriving from the tough Mojave portion of the road or preparing themselves for the dreaded desert journey. The El Rancho provided excellent facilities, and the motel was regularly filled to capacity. Originally the El Rancho contained 50 rooms, but at its peak it featured 101 rooms, 26 of them with kitchenettes. In 1947 room rates started at $4.50 a night for a single bed and went up from there. A 100-foot-tall neon sign later erected on the property became a beacon that could be seen for miles.

In 1979 the motel was closed to the public and rented exclusively by the Santa Fe Railway and its employees. When Interstates 15 and 40 were completed, newer and more convenient motels were built alongside the new highways, and the El Rancho slowly fell into disrepair. In 1987 Rick Byers bought the property and began the process of restoration. It was reopened only to close five years later, again deteriorating due to hard times and poor management. In 1994 Byers repurchased the property and sunk another $300,000 into a second restoration, which included a Route 66 Visitor's Center adjacent to the motel office. Unfortunately, current traffic on Historic Route 66 did not generate sufficient business to justify keeping the motel well maintained, and once again it is headed on a downward slide.

BARSTOW
c. 1948

More than 150 miles of harsh, sun-baked terrain awaited motorists departing Needles for Barstow. Previously known as Waterman, the town's name was changed in 1886 to honor Santa Fe President William Barstow Strong after that railroad built a depot in town. (His middle name was used because Kansas already had a "Strong" station on the line.) A new railroad depot, Casa del Desierto, completed in 1911, was added to the National Register of Historic Places in 1975. Today, the beautifully restored "House in the Desert" is home to the Route 66 Mother Road Museum (www.Barstow66museum.itgo.com).

During Barstow's early years the town was located on the north side of the railroad tracks but as a result of frequent expansion of the railroad, was eventually relocated to the south. Four-lane Interstate 15 was completed from Barstow to Victorville in 1958, shortening the distance between the two towns by 5 miles. The bypass, as elsewhere, had a tremendous negative impact on Barstow's downtown business district, but the city found new life at its eastern edge. There, the intersection of Interstate 40 and Interstate 15 functions as an ideal refueling point and rest stop.

VICTORVILLE
c. 1939

The small town of Victorville is located 97 miles northeast of Los Angeles at the western edge of the Mojave Desert. In 1885, the Southern California Railroad built a station there and the area became known as Huntington Station. It was later dubbed "Victor" after the railroad's construction superintendent, Jacob Nash Victor, then renamed Victorville when the mail service began confusing Victor, California, with Victor, Colorado. Victorville, a favorite location for filming western "B movies" in the 1960s, has survived and grown since the Interstate totally bypassed the town in 1972, as is evidenced by the population increase from 11,200 in 1972 to 71,224 today. At the time the above postcard photograph was taken, the city's population was listed as approximately 2,500.

Route 66 ran west through Victorville on D Street, making a right turn onto 7th Street, and continuing through town toward the steep grade of the Cajon Pass on its way to San Bernardino before terminating in Los Angeles. The popular California Route 66 Museum (www.califrt66museum.org) is located on Route 66 in "Old Town" Victorville and is housed in the onetime Red Rooster Café building, where *The Jazz Singer*, starring Neil Diamond, was filmed.

GREEN SPOT MOTEL, VICTORVILLE
c. 1947

Heading west through Victorville, the path of Highway 66 ran down D Street until reaching Seventh Street, where the Mother Road took a rare 90-degree turn and continued on through town. One block after the turn, near the corner of Seventh and C Streets, sits the landmark Green Spot Motel. In its heyday Victorville served as backdrop for hundreds of Hollywood Westerns and as a getaway for the stars. The Green Spot Motel was the crème de la crème. The motel consisted of 20 gable-roofed buildings, each containing two guest units with flat-roofed carports connecting them. The buildings were arranged in a U shape with 10 across the rear and 5 along each side. In the center was a magnificently landscaped courtyard that later contained a swimming pool.

The Green Spot was at one time part of the United Auto Courts system and billed as "Truly De Luxe." A café, also called the Green Spot, was located on the corner of C Street and Seventh. Very popular in its day, the café was frequented by many a celebrity. Orson Welles was rumored to have written much of his material in one of the booths. In 1953 the Green Spot Café burned to the ground.

After the interstate bypass was built in 1972, the motel began the typical decline and soon became home to drug dealing and prostitution. In 1982, the 1940s star Kay Aldridge, best known for her portrayal of Nyoka in the serial *Perils of Nyoka*, married Harry Nasland, who was then part owner of the Green Spot Motel. He died after a few months of marriage, and Aldridge inherited his interest in the motel. She vowed to clean up the place and restore it to its original splendor as a premier getaway and rest stop. It was more than she could handle. She eventually became disillusioned and moved to Maine. A plaque located on the front wall next to the entrance arch reads "Nyoka's Hideaway," bearing witness to her fondness for the Green Spot.

Aldridge sold the motel to Benjamin Wu and Nancy Wei, who operated it until 1995. Aldridge died of a heart attack on January 12, 1995, and two months later Wei was sentenced to 13 years in prison for shooting and killing her husband. Aldridge's estate foreclosed on the property, and the Green Spot sat dormant. It was eventually sold to Hemant Patel in 2001. The Green Spot Motel currently rents to weekly and monthly tenants and is showing signs of a slight recovery.

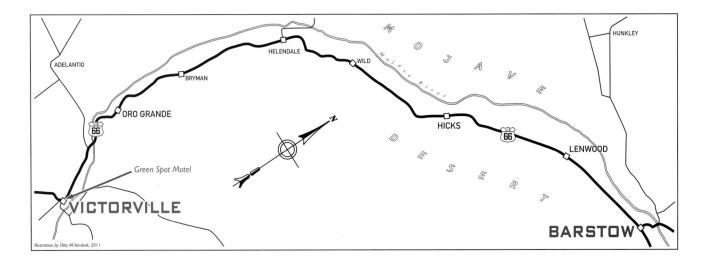

Illustration by Otto M. Vondrak, 2011

THE OUTPOST, PHELAN
c. 1952

In 1928, at the junction of U.S. Highway 66 and U.S. 395, a café and fuel stop known as The Outpost began serving up food and gas to travelers brave enough to challenge the primitive road conditions of the time. The Outpost served travelers through the Great Depression, World War II, and beyond into the glory days of Route 66.

In 1961, the Newton family purchased the business, which at the time was operating on weekends only. According to George Newton, traffic was so slow in those days you could "shoot a cannon off on Route 66 and not hit anything." Inside, the café had five small tables and counter space for seven customers. A jukebox sat in the corner, providing music and entertainment for a nickel.

Soon after the purchase, plans were underway to modernize and widen the roadway to interstate standards. Unfortunately, The Outpost sat on land needed for this upgrade. The state filed eminent domain and offered $600 to the Newtons for the land. Unhappy with the offer, the Newtons took the case to court, which agreed with the Newtons and awarded enough compensation for the family to build a new facility not far from the original. The new and improved version of The Outpost opened and began serving customers in 1964.

The building that once housed The Outpost café was never torn down. The state sold it to Donna Wyatt who turned it into a wedding chapel dubbed The Outpost Wedding Chapel. This business was the last to occupy the building.

The opening of the new café and gas station coincided with the opening of the new interstate. Although business began to pick up, George recalls "conditions were very primitive back then. We had to haul water by truck twice a day from Victorville." George also remembers that the electricity was not very reliable and that it often went out completely when it snowed. "We had to ask customers to turn on their headlights and point them into the café so we could see," says George.

Today, The Outpost is known as Newton's The Outpost, a full-service gas station/truck stop that includes a restaurant/café with seating for 110 customers, a driver's lounge, showers, laundromat, a dump station, and more. George laughs at the fact that The Outpost has been in three different cities over the years "without moving a brick." Because of U.S. Postal Service zoning, Newton's The Outpost has been in Phelan and Hesperia, and currently resides in Oak Hills. Amid all the changes, the most important aspects of The Outpost have remained rock solid: hospitality and good food.

SUMMIT INN, CAJON SUMMIT
c. 1957

The Summit Inn was built in 1952 by Burton and Dorothy Riley on what was then two-lane Route 66. The roadbed sat on the east side of the restaurant at the time of the hotel's construction, but was moved in 1955 to its current location on the west side when it was upgraded to four-lane status. The restaurant sat on the west side of the road when C. A. Stevens purchased the business from the Rileys on October 13, 1966. Stevens has owned and operated it ever since.

In 1969 and 1970, Interstate 15 obliterated the Mother Road in this area, but the Summit Inn survived the changes and continues to serve good road fare. In 1969 Stevens moved the service station end of the business closer to the off-ramp that was being built as part of the new interstate upgrade. As late as 1972, water had to be hauled to the Summit Inn by truck and was pumped into the restaurant from a storage tank located alongside the restaurant.

When Stevens bought the business, he also acquired a waitress by the name of Hilda Fish, who continued working at the Summit Inn until retirement in 2002. During the late 1980s, representatives of the Denny's Corporation approached Stevens with an offer to convert the restaurant. When Stevens asked Fish what she thought of the idea, she responded, "You put a Denny's here and I quit." The Denny's was never built, and Fish stayed.

The Summit Inn continues to be a popular stop on the Cajon Pass—so popular that even the King himself, Elvis Presley, was reported to have paid a visit. According to Fish, Elvis stopped at the Summit Inn one night, but left hurriedly when he saw that none of his records were in the jukebox. It's true—Elvis *has* left the building.

BONO'S, FONTANA
c. 1950

On July 17, 1936, Mr. and Mrs. Jim Bono opened a small orange juice stand along Route 66 in Fontana. Although it was a modest beginning, bigger and better things were to come. The Bono family migrated to the area because Jim and his father, Joe, had a dream of growing and harvesting grapes. The region around Fontana and Cucamonga was known to provide "some of the finest grapes in the world" according to Jim's son, Joe (named for his grandfather.)

Fruit stands were a common sight along this stretch of Route 66. The area was loaded with orange groves and every grove and farm had an orange juice stand. Bono's stand sold "all you can drink" orange juice for 10 cents a glass, as well as bulk wine, which sold for 99 cents a jug. Crates of oranges could be had for a dollar and sold like hot cakes. Olives and honey were also among the better selling products. Tourists heading back East were especially fond of the crated oranges as they were able to bring a bit sunny of California

home with them. As popularity grew, the business expanded to include a deli offering Italian foods and specialties.

In 1950, Bono's began selling prepared food to go. The idea, according to Joe Bono, was to get people shopping in the deli while they waited for their food to be prepared. As their reputation grew, the business expanded to include a sit-down restaurant with a capacity of 135 diners. By the mid- to late 1950s, Bono's was the premier Italian restaurant in the area. People came from miles around to sample the specially prepared authentic Italian dishes. When the freeways and interstates came through and replaced old Route 66, Bono's did not miss a beat, continuing to serve food to a loyal clientele. It wasn't until the 1990s that business slowed and the doors closed.

Just mentioning Bono's surely triggers a watering mouth for anyone who has ever enjoyed a meal there. Unfortunately, Bono's is currently open only for special occasions and parties.

PASADENA
c. 1958

Spaniards established themselves in the region around present-day Pasadena as early as the mid-1700s. Prior to that, Hahamonga Indians inhabited the region and were eventually enslaved by the conquering Spaniards.

Modern-day Pasadena owes its origin to Daniel Berry, who along with a group of friends, desperately sought to escape the bitterly cold Indiana winters. On September 12, 1873, Berry chose the land of Rancho San Pasqual at the foot of the San Gabriel Mountains for their yearly retreat. This group from Indiana was also responsible for naming the city—Pasadena is a Chippewa word meaning "crown of the valley."

Pasadena incorporated and became an official city on June 19, 1886, and soon evolved into a retreat and playground for well-to-do folks from the Midwest and East who gathered there in the winter months.

In 1926, U.S. Highway 66 came through town via Colorado Boulevard and continued toward Los Angeles via Fair Oaks Avenue and Huntington Drive, finally reaching Broadway and ending at 7th Street in downtown Los Angeles. As many as four other alignments through and westward out of Pasadena took place over the lifetime of Route 66.

One cannot think of Pasadena without thinking, too, of the famous Rose Bowl and the Tournament of Roses Parade. The first parade took place on January 1, 1890, but was first sponsored by the Tournament of Roses Association in 1898. The annual event travels down a portion of Colorado Boulevard, the path that once carried Route 66.

During the golden age of Route 66, Colorado Boulevard through Pasadena was lined with dozens of cafés and motels catering to tourists. As time and progress pushed forward, these motels and tourist facilities slowly disappeared one by one. With each passing year, we move toward a time when all will be but a faded memory.

FIGUEROA STREET TUNNELS/ARROYO SECO PARKWAY, LOS ANGELES
c. 1943

Construction of three of the four Figueroa Street Tunnels was completed in 1931, and the fourth and final tunnel was completed in 1936. That same year saw Route 66 rerouted through the tunnels. The downtown Los Angeles terminus at Broadway and Seventh changed to Olympic and Lincoln Boulevard in Santa Monica and was reached via Sunset Boulevard and Santa Monica Boulevard.

Construction of the Arroyo Seco Parkway, extending from Pasadena en route to Los Angeles, began in 1938. December 30, 1940, saw the completion and opening of the beautiful, groundbreaking parkway. This Highway 66 bypass alignment was considered to be the first freeway west of the Mississippi. In 1942 two-way traffic through the Figueroa Tunnels was altered to handle one-way, northbound traffic, and the Arroyo Seco Parkway/Route 66 was extended toward downtown Los Angeles to include the Figueroa Street Tunnels.

Today, although Arroyo Seco Parkway is a beautiful drive, safety is a big concern. When dedicated, parkway speeds were set at a maximum of 45 miles per hour. With tight curves, narrow lanes, lack of shoulder space, and very little room for entering and exiting, traveling at today's speeds makes navigating the parkway somewhat challenging. It is now listed as a National Scenic Byway and is well worth the effort to explore its historic path.

PARADISE MOTEL, LOS ANGELES
c. 1946

In 1946, Los Angeles resident Harvey R. Hansen began constructing a new motel. It would be called the Paradise Motel, which reflected Hansen's view on the climate and landscape of Southern California. Nestled beneath a small hill at the corner of Sunset Boulevard and Beaudry Avenue, the Paradise Motel was advertised as "In the Center of Los Angeles and Everything"—just minutes from downtown, Hollywood, historic Olvera Street, and Chinatown. The back of the postcard also claims the Pacific Ocean is only 15 minutes away—quite possible in 1946, but a far-out fantasy today.

The Paradise was built of stucco and designed to form the typical L shape. It offered 19 guest rooms and 1 apartment that served as living quarters for the manager. The corner of Sunset and Beaudry also featured a full-service Texaco station that eventually was closed and replaced by a larger building housing a medical center that still exists.

In 1963, a purple neon sign outlining the word "Paradise" was installed under the existing motel sign and over the office. The existing motel sign and the motel buildings were also outlined in purple at the same time by the National Neon Products Company. Today that neon can still be seen at night from blocks away, casting an eerie, unearthly glow to the property.

Occasionally the Paradise Motel is featured in movies and commercials, but even the movie crews tell me that this is a rough place and should be avoided at night.

When in Los Angeles ~

"Paradise Motel"

1116 Sunset Blvd.
MA-dison 4569

Where Hwy. 6-66 crosses 101

414

Sources

Books

Curtis, C. H. *The Missouri U.S. 66 Tour Book*. St. Louis, Mo.: D. I. Enterprises, 1994.

Graham, Shellee. *Tales from the Coral Court: Photos & Stories from a Lost Route 66 Landmark*. St. Louis, Mo.: Virginia Publishing, 2000.

Noe, Sally. *66 Sights on Route 66*. Gallup, N.M.: Gallup Downtown Development Group, 1992.

Piotrowski, Scott. *Finding the End of the Mother Road*. Pasadena, Calif.: 66 Productions, 2003.

Repp, Thomas Arthur. *Route 66: The Empires of Amusement*. Lynwood, Wash.: Mock Turtle Press, 1999.

——. *Route 66: The Romance of the West*. Lynwood, Wash.: Mock Turtle Press, 2002.

Rittenhouse, Jack D. *A Guide Book to Highway 66*. (Reprint of 1946 printing.) Albuquerque: University of New Mexico Press, 1989.

Ross, Jim. *Oklahoma Route 66*. Arcadia, Okla.: Ghost Town Press, 2001.

Schneider, Jill. *Route 66 Across New Mexico: A Wanderer's Guide*. Albuquerque: University of New Mexico Press, 1991.

Scott, Quinta and Susan Croce Kelly. *Route 66: The Highway and its People*. Norman: University of Oklahoma Press, 1988.

——. *Along Route 66*. Norman: University of Oklahoma Press, 2000.

Snyder, Tom. *The Route 66 Traveler's Companion*. New York: St. Martin's Press, 1990.

Teague, Thomas. *Searching for 66*. Springfield, Ill.: Samizdat House, 1991.

Wallis, Michael. *Route 66: The Mother Road*. New York: St. Martin's Press, 1990.

Weis, John. *Traveling the New, Historic Route 66 of Illinois*. Frankfort, Ill.: A. O. Motivation Programs, 1997.

Witzel, Michael Karl. *Route 66 Remembered*. Osceola, Wis.: Motorbooks International, 1996.

Periodicals

National Historic Route 66 Federation News (www.national66.org), 1995–present.

Route 66 Magazine (www.route66magazine.com), 1993–present.

Wallace, Norman. "The Scenic Wonderland Highway." *Arizona Highways*, May 1955.

Interviews

Adam, Nick. Ariston Café, Litchfield, Ill.

Alderson, Jace. Sands Motel, Moriarty, N.M.

Bannister, George. Copper State Court, Ash Fork, Ariz.

Berger, Lois. Log Cabin Lodge, Gallup, N.M.

Brace, Frank and Susan. Arcadia Lodge, Kingman, Ariz.

Bravo, Luis. Palms Motel, Needles, Calif.

Delgadillo, Robert. Snow Cap, Seligman, Ariz.

Edmunds, Dub. Jesse's Café/Mid-Point Café, Adrian, Tex.

Edwards, Ernie. Ernie's Pig Hip, Broadwell, Ill.

Ferguson, John. Boots Motel, Carthage, Mo.

Goodridge, Edward. Vernelle's Motel, Newburg, Mo.

Hauser, Fran. Mid-Point Café, Adrian, Tex.

Kraft, Bob. The Riviera, Gardner, Ill.

Krieger, Karen. El Trovatore, Kingman, Ariz.

Lehman, Ramona. Munger-Moss Motel, Lebanon, Mo.

Manker, Gina. Log Cabin Inn, Pontiac, Ill.

McPherson, Olind. Rut's Corner Café, Litchfield, Ill.

Miller, Atholl "Jiggs." Devils Elbow, Mo.

Mudd, Roy. Wagon Wheel Motel, Cuba, Mo.

Murphy, Lorie. Shady Rest Court, West Tulsa, Okla.

Natha, Mohamed. Aztec Motel, Albuquerque, N.M.

Noe, Sally. Thoreau, N.M.

Patel, Jack. Desert Hills Motel, Tulsa, Okla.

Patel, Suresh. Luna Lodge, Albuquerque, N.M.

Pendya, Mr. Rest Haven Motor Court, Springfield, Mo.

Radosevich, John. Johnnie's Café, Thoreau, N.M.

Rhea, Patrick. Dell Rhea's Chicken Basket, Willowbrook, Ill.

Roberts, Teresa. Pioneer Motel, Springfield, Ill.

Sanchez Jr., Canuto. Lakeview Courts, Santa Rosa, N.M.

Stevens, C. A. Summit Inn, Cajon Pass, Calif.

Stevens, Les. Steve's Café, Chenoa, Ill.

Vaidya, San. Downtowner Motel, Williams, Ariz.

Vidas, Zora. Wishing Well Motel, LaGrange, Ill.

Waldmire, Sue. Cozy Dog, Springfield, Ill.

Werth, Wilfred. Redwood Motel, Lincoln, Ill.

Whaley, Tresa. Vega Motel, Vega, Tex.

Wheatley, Betty. Avon Courts/Buffalo Ranch, Afton, Okla.

Young, Alan. Luna Café, Mitchell, Ill.

INDEX